THE WAY OF LIFE SERIES

(*A Series of the International Studies Conference*)

THE PAKISTANI
WAY OF LIFE

Other Titles in this Series

THE AUSTRALIAN WAY OF LIFE *edited by* George Caiger

THE SOUTH AFRICAN WAY OF LIFE *edited by* G. H. Calpin

THE BRITISH WAY OF LIFE *by* K. B. Smellie

THE NORWEGIAN WAY OF LIFE *by* Frede Castberg

The Great Mosque at Lahore, Built by the Emperor Aurangzib in the 17th Century

Frontispiece.

THE PAKISTANI
WAY OF LIFE

BY

ISHTIAQ HUSAIN QURESHI

REVISED EDITION

FREDERICK A. PRAEGER
NEW YORK

DS
379
.Q7
1956

This volume of the Way of Life Series has been prepared under the auspices of the International Studies Conference, on the request of U. N. E. S. C. O.

PUBLISHED IN 1956 IN THE UNITED STATES OF AMERICA BY FREDERICK A. PRAEGER, INC., PUBLISHERS, 150 EAST 52ND STREET, NEW YORK 22, N.Y.

SECOND EDITION, REVISED

LIBRARY OF CONGRESS CATALOG CARD NUMBER 56-7745

975.47
Q9p
1956

PRINTED IN GREAT BRITAIN

Contents

CHAPTER   PAGE

FOREWORD ix

PREFACE TO THE FIRST EDITION xi

PREFACE TO THE SECOND EDITION xi

I   THE PAKISTANI NATION 1

II   THE FAMILY 17

III   EDUCATIONAL SYSTEM 24

IV   POLITICAL INSTITUTIONS AND ASPIRATIONS 35

V   ECONOMIC INSTITUTIONS AND ASPIRATIONS 47

VI   RELIGIOUS INSTITUTIONS AND ASPIRATIONS 61

VII   THE PAKISTANI PEOPLE AND THE WORLD 69

APPENDIX : The Present State of Scientific Research on the questions raised above, with Succinct Bibliography 75

SELECT BIBLIOGRAPHY 77

INDEX 9

List of Plates

The Great Mosque at Lahore   *Frontispiece*

FACING PAGE

1. A sailor of Chittagong   4
2. A Sindhi   4
3. A Pathan patriarch   4
4. A Punjabi   4
5. A Punjabi village woman churning milk   5
6. The courtyard of a Pathan house   5
7. An art student   20
8. A Pakistani girl dressed for tennis   20
9. A Punjabi village girl   20
10. An urban family at dinner   21
11. A popular tea shop in the suburbs of Karachi   21
12. A labourers' village in the suburbs of Karachi   26
13. A fruit vendor's shop in Peshawar   26
14. School children at exercise   27
15. Students of botany in their classroom   27
16. Karachi: the business centre   36
17. A part of the Punjab University   36
18. A bargain amongst the Pathans   37
19. Fishing in Eastern Pakistan   37
20. A hill man ploughing his fields   52
21. A harvest scene   52
22. Jute being taken for baling   53
23. Cotton being brought to a mill   53

Foreword

IGNORANCE is the fruitful mother of misunderstanding, and it is in the hope that fuller knowledge may make for fuller co-operation that this series of monographs is being issued. The various authors were selected and invited to write by an international committee, but it must be clearly stated that the treatises are in no sense official. Every author writes on his own responsibility and from his own point of view : in no case is he the nominee or official spokesman of any government, still less of any party. That a treatise on Pakistan should be among the first to appear is a matter of chance, but we may feel that it is a happy chance.

The author, Dr. Qureshi, has written several books on History, Politics and Religion; has been Professor of History in the University of Lahore; is a member of the Constituent Assembly and of the Council of the Pakistan Institute of International Affairs, and now Minister for Education in the Government of Pakistan. It is very plain then that he does not write from an ivory tower or a professorial armchair : he tells us of events *quorum pars magna fuit.*

He has a stirring tale to tell of the efforts of a country which so lately as 1947 started, as he says, from scratch—with no organized government, no secretariat, or even the tables and chairs and stationery for one; with most of the merchants and industrial workers gone from the country, and refugees by millions pouring in. Writing with enthusiasm, but without bitterness and without fanaticism, he tells how order was brought out of chaos, and gives the impression, only a few years later, of a country abounding with life and vigour. By the quality of his first chapter and his last he achieves very successfully the object of such a book; he leaves the reader wanting to know more.

A. L. IRVINE

Preface to the First Edition

THE difficulties inherent in writing about a nation which achieved statehood only a few years ago are obvious; they are further enhanced by the fact that its habitat had to be carved out of a sub-continent which had been governed by a foreign power as a single political and geographical entity for more than a century. The representatives of the Pakistani nation are, even now, busy in drafting a constitution which will create some new institutions and alter a number of those which already exist. Many political and social adjustments will come in the wake of the changes in the organs of government; revolutionary forces in the realms of social and economic reconstruction set into motion by freedom have only begun to work. The fate of Kashmir still remains undecided. This treatise, therefore, necessarily resembles the *critique* of a canvas which is still incomplete.

The author has not been a mere spectator of this mighty drama. Not even the humblest can remain unaffected by mighty tremors which shake a sub-continent; revolutions do not breed hermits. It would, therefore, be idle to claim that his feelings have not been involved, but he has tried his best to achieve objectivity. Perhaps the fact that he has been in the thick of the mêlée has given him information and insight which mere detachment could not bestow.

I. H. QURESHI

KARACHI.

Preface to the Second Edition

THE second Constituent Assembly of Pakistan has enacted a constitution which is now in force; it was, therefore, necessary to revise the book for a second edition. The rest of the information, including statistical data, has also been brought up to date.

I. H. QURESHI

February, 1957.

CHAPTER I

The Pakistani Nation

A GLANCE at the map of Pakistan will show that it consists of two regions separated from each other by more than a thousand miles of Indian territory. Western Pakistan has an area of 306,860 square miles and consists of the province of West Pakistan and the Federal Capital. Eastern Pakistan has an area of 53,920 square miles and consists of a single province—East Pakistan. The population of Western Pakistan is 33,779,000 and the dominant racial type is Scytho-Aryan. East Pakistan has a population of 42,063,000, the dominant racial type being Dravido-Mongoloid. There are obvious Semitic traces in the people of the North-West Frontier while the Baluchis are predominantly Aryan. The Aryan traits are more obvious among the people of Western Pakistan and the Dravidian among the population of Eastern Pakistan.

The people are further divided into linguistic groups. The main languages spoken in well-defined areas are Panjabi, Pushtu, Baluchi, Sindhi, Makrani and Bengali. These languages derive their names from the regions in which they are spoken. Panjabi is the language of the West Punjab, Baluchi of South Baluchistan, Sindhi of Sind, Makrani of Makran—which is situated on the borders of Iran—and Bengali is spoken in East Bengal. Pushtu or Pukhtu is the language of the Pukhtun, the Pathan. All these languages belong to the Aryan group. The only exception is Brohi, spoken by some Baluchis, which provides a small Dravidian linguistic island. The languages of Western Pakistan have a large percentage of Persian and Arabic words; Bengali is more Sanskritic. Makrani and Baluchi are more akin to Persian than to any other language. A large number of refugees speak only Urdu, which serves as *lingua franca* throughout Pakistan. In the greater part of Western Pakistan, Urdu is also the vehicle of literary and

scientific thought, though some of the regional languages also
have considerable literature, mostly religious, poetical or
fictional. In Eastern Pakistan, Urdu is less widely used, but it
is understood and spoken in all urban areas. The national
language of Western Pakistan is, therefore, Urdu, though there
exists considerable sentimental attachment to the local languages
as well. Of the latter, Panjabi is almost a dialect of Urdu. The
common stock of a large percentage of Arabic and Persian words
makes it easy for those who know one of the languages to learn
another. Most people in Pakistan are bi-lingual, speaking their
regional language and Urdu with almost equal facility. The
educated classes are at least tri-lingual, speaking quite easily a
regional language, Urdu and English. Quite a large number know
Persian or Arabic also as a matter of course.

Each linguistic group possesses some peculiar characteristics in
social customs, food and even natural predilections. For instance,
the people of Eastern Pakistan are rice-eating and fish forms an
important element of their food. Wheat is the staple food of the
people of Western Pakistan. The Pathan of the North-West
Frontier eats well, his diet consisting of, in addition to wheat
bread, rich mutton provided by the fat-tailed sheep and luscious
fruits in which the province abounds. The Pathan owes his
splendid physique to his dry and healthy climate and the quality
of his well-balanced and nourishing diet. The Panjabi eats less
meat but he is exceedingly fond of milk and milk products. Milk,
butter and curds form a good percentage of his daily diet and he
quenches his thirst with skimmed milk, of which he drinks large
quantities diluted with water. The Panjabi is also well-built,
healthy and active. The Sindhi resembles the Panjabi in his
dietary habits, the difference being mainly in the way of cooking.
The Baluch is more akin to the Pathan, though he differs from
him in habits and outlook on life.

Generally speaking, the people of Western Pakistan have a
good physique and make excellent agriculturists and soldiers.
They are capable of sustained hard work and possess great
courage combined with a sense of discipline. A large portion of
the so-called Indian armies under the British was drawn from
Western Pakistan and these soldiers have been admired whereso-
ever they have fought. The Bengali, living in a damp and water-

logged warm climate, not subjected to the same extremes of heat and cold, does not possess such a good physique, nor is he so warlike. He is peace-loving and dislikes a quarrel involving violence. There are certain exceptions, however. The people of the district of Mymensingh are known for their physical strength and warlike propensities. Interspersed in the population are the descendants of Turkish and Afghan settlers who have not forgotten their traditions. When roused, the Muslims of East Bengal are capable of giving a good account of themselves as fighters. The *jihad* movement led by Saiyid Ahmad Shahid against the Sikh kingdom of Lahore in the 19th century drew a fair number of recruits from the Muslims of Bengal. The British discouraged the recruitment of the Bengalis to their armies for political reasons. Now the Bengalis are again taking an interest in military training. They have a special aptitude for the navy and make good sailors. As the province is divided by mighty rivers and communications are difficult, the Bengali often cultivates an insular outlook. The Pathan is warlike and fond of a good fight. He continued an unequal struggle against the British for more than a century to maintain his independence and was never completely subdued. He has developed, in the course of history, through his sustained struggles against various empires created on the soil of neighbouring lands, such qualities of courage, endurance and skill in fighting that he has become the best guerrilla soldier of the world. His bravery and chivalry, hospitality and generosity, tenacity and freedom from fear are matchless. He possesses a quixotic sense of honour. He was always a problem for the British, because nothing could reconcile him to foreign domination. To-day he is an asset to Pakistan, finding a fulfilment of his long struggle in the establishment of a Muslim State wherein he himself defines the limits of his liberty as a full partner in the governance of his area as well as the country. He is not averse to peaceful pursuits, and is now demanding his full share of education, vocational training, industrialization and agricultural development so that he may reap the fullest advantage from his newly-won freedom.

The Panjabi is educationally ahead of other groups. He has an essentially practical outlook and makes an excellent scientific researcher, mechanic or agriculturist. His fighting qualities as a regular soldier, when properly trained and officered, are well known. As a peaceful citizen, he is industrious, progressive and law-abiding. The Baluchis living in their vast expanses of cool deserts and cultivating the oases to yield them sustenance have a large percentage of nomads among them but those who have settled down are industrious agriculturists. They also have excellent fighting qualities. The Sindhis are like the Panjabis, but they are not so progressive or educated, having been hitherto kept backward by their Hindu compatriots who had monopolized trade, industry and education in Sind under the British and formed the bulk of the land-owners, the Sindhi Muslims providing mostly unskilled labour and acting as tenants at will. To-day conditions are different because most of the Hindus have migrated to India. To these may be added a large number of refugees from India who have greater traditions of polished refinement in their speech and tastes and who are mostly traders, teachers, artisans, craftsmen and public servants.

Thus it will be clear that every linguistic group has certain well-defined characteristics and differs from others considerably.

The diversity is, however, not so great as to create fissiparous tendencies. The people are fully conscious of a common nationality. This feeling of unity is mainly based on religious, historical, geographical and political factors. Islam is a great unifying factor and the population is overwhelmingly Muslim. In the Indo-Pakistan sub-continent, the Muslims share a common history. They treasure the same memories of glorious victories won by their ancestors against overwhelming odds in this sub-continent, of great cultural achievement, of undoubted success in establishing a government among an alien people which gave the conqueror and the conquered alike peace, prosperity and scope for development, and of defending themselves and those who came under their protection from the ravages and inroads of barbarous invaders. They share the memory of the humiliation to which they were subjected as the result of their failure to hold together, so that they could not suppress internal revolt or external aggression which ultimately resulted in the loss not only of their dominion over the sub-continent of India but also in their own subjugation; nor have they forgotten the fact that they were treated with hostility in every walk of life by the dominant com-

1. A Sailor of Chittagong
   (East Pakistan)

2. A Sindhi

3. A Pathan Patriarch

4. A Punjabi

5. A Punjabi Village Woman Churning Milk for Butter

6. The Courtyard of a Pathan House. The Men are Good Fighters and a Gun is a Prized Possession

munity living in the sub-continent, simply because they believed in Islam. Geographical proximity has brought even greater similarity than exists between them and other Muslim peoples all over the world. Western Pakistan is a geographical unit, consisting of the basin of the River Indus and its tributaries and the hilly regions which form its western and northern bulwarks. From time immemorial traders have used its great waterways for trade and commerce, thus creating community of thought and interest; its railways also have followed the course of the rivers. Politically these groups, too small to organize themselves into separate states, are fully aware of the proximity of large states on their borders and, therefore, are happy in equal partnership and democratic unity. Indeed the variety which characterizes the various ethnical groups is not of the type which creates deep divisions; its very slightness adds strength to the intensity of a common patriotism which makes the Pakistani nation. The most binding force is spiritual and cultural unity; hence it is necessary to give a short history of the growth of a common and distinct culture which has created the Pakistani nation.

The homogeneity of all Islamic peoples is a most striking feature of the influence of Islam; a common idealism has not only affected their outlook on life, it has fashioned its very pattern. Islam does not divide life into watertight compartments; it claims the entire allegiance of its followers. Hence it is all-pervading in character and affects all aspects of human activity. As a consequence, the uniformity of all Muslim peoples is far more striking than their diversity. This is true, to a remarkable extent, of Muslims of the Indo-Pakistan sub-continent as well; the impress of Islam on them is deep and real, and they are no unworthy members of the large Muslim fraternity. Their outlook on life, their way of living, their tastes and inclinations are essentially Muslim and their long domicile among a people with different outlook, traditions and culture has not affected the essentially Muslim characteristics of Indian Islam. If the preponderant un-Islamic influence played any part, it was in putting the Indian Muslim on his guard and making him more conscious of the need of preserving his heritage from being engulfed in the rising tide of resurgent Hinduism. Thus it would be futile to try to find any fundamental difference in creed or in the code of social and individual behaviour between Indian Islam and Islam in other regions; yet it would be an exaggeration to say that the Indian Muslims did not possess a strong individuality.

This individuality was rooted in the catholicity of Islam. It may sound paradoxical, yet it is a fact that on the one hand Islam claims the entire allegiance of man and on the other it leaves a vast field of human activity free from all shackles. Where the mind would benefit from following its own inclinations and exploring new avenues, it has been left free. It was this freedom which resulted in the creative tendencies of Muslim civilization and laid the foundations of scientific objectivity in the thought of the world. Before Spanish intolerance in the West and Mongol fury in the East destroyed important centres of Islamic culture, Islam had held aloft the torch of inquiry and learning. The decadence brought about by the loss of trade and territory dried up the very fountains of Muslim thought-streams and produced stagnation, which erroneously came to be identified with Islam itself in the popular mind. When Islam entered India, it was, in spite of approaching decadence, still virile. It had not lost its spirit of inquiry, its insatiable thirst for knowledge, its childlike inquisitiveness. Muslims in India started with a clean slate. They did not suffer from any complexes regarding race or colour. Within the fold of Islam the Negro and the European, the Arab and the Dravidian were alike. Every convert was a brother, every human being was worthy of conversion, hence all races and peoples were equal in the sight of the Muslim. The pride of the conqueror was softened by the desire to bring the conquered into the camp of Islam. The Muslim was proud of Islam and its ideology, but not of his race. Racially the conquered Hindu was different, but not inferior. Hence the noblest in the realm, even the monarchs, did not disdain to marry Hindu maidens, who accepted the religion of their husbands but could not wipe out all traces of their culture and thought. Nor was there any desire among the Muslims that their Hindu wives should forget their entire past; they tolerated traces of Hindu traditions so far as they did not come into conflict with Islam.

Muslim tolerance, inquisitiveness and social catholicity produced the right atmosphere for cultural contacts with the Hindus, who themselves were inheritors of a hoary civilization. Even before the conquest of India by Muslims, the Arabs had trade and cultural relations with the Hindus. When Muhammad bin Qasim (8th century A.D.) conquered Sind, this contact increased, and Arab geographers and writers were interested in the land of the Indus. The Abbasids, the period of whose glory was the apogee of cultural progress in Eastern Islam, held liberal views about the learning and sciences of other nations and the Jew, the Greek, the Hindu were alike welcome in their courts if they had some contribution to make. The famous Barmecides were themselves of Buddhist origin. This catholic tradition was inherited by the Turkish conquerors of India and maintained by them throughout their rule. When Mahmud's armies were penetrating farther and farther (11th century), the famous Alberuni was carrying on patient research in India which he incorporated in his well-known book *Kitab-ul-Hind* (Book of India). It would be difficult to find a more sympathetic, thoroughgoing, correct and impartial compendium of information written about an alien people by any scholar whose own outlook on life was so utterly different. Amir Khusraw (14th century), a Turk of mixed parentage and one of the greatest figures in the realm of Persian literature and poetry, assiduously cultivated a taste for Hindu culture. His glowing descriptions of Hindu learning, his devotion to Hindu music and his understanding of Hindu ethics all show his regard for the Hindu outlook on life. Firuz Shah (14th century), Sikandar Lodi (15th century), Akbar (16th century) and various other monarchs employed scholars to translate Sanskrit works into Persian. Muslim poets sometimes wrote Hindi poetry and Malik Muhammad Ja'isi, Abdur Rahim Khan Khanan and Kabir rank among the greatest of Hindi poets. The impact with Islam brought about a great renaissance in Hinduism which resulted in the great Bhakti movement.

All this shows that there was great cultural contact between the Muslims and the Hindus, and the Muslims, while firmly relying on the truth of Islam and fully conscious of the greatness of their own culture and tradition, were not averse to the adoption of such features of Hindu culture as could be brought into harmony with their idealism and needs. Anything which was antagonistic to their beliefs or ideas was severely discarded. The Muslims in India never permitted any impurities to creep into their doctrine, nor did they allow their new environment to affect their orientation. They were helped in this effort by the great contrast between Islam and Hinduism. The result was that the process of assimilation of Hindu characteristics by Indian Islam was confined to the mere superficialities of life. In all deeper matters, the Indian Muslim was no different from other Muslims. The only exception was of the language. For theological and academic purposes, Arabic was used; the language of the administration was Persian, and as the rulers were mostly of Turkish origin, the use of Turkish was never given up by the court. But their close contact with the people brought into existence a new language, which adopted the grammatical structure of the Prakritic language of North India and retained a large percentage of Arabic, Persian and Turkish words. This language was sometimes called Urdu (the language of the camp) and sometimes Hindwi (the language of the Hindus). Hindu scholars had taken up the study of Persian and Arabic fairly early; indeed we hear of Hindu professors lecturing in Muslim colleges in the thirteenth century. Under Sikandar Lodi (15th century) we find that education in Arabic and Persian became extensively popular among the Hindus. From the very beginning the Hindus had supplied the majority of the revenue bureaucracy of the Muslim Empire; they soon discovered that their prospects of promotion were greatly advanced by the ability to read and write Persian. This movement was so advanced by the time that Akbar came to the throne that he abolished the system of duplicate registers in the local sub-divisions where accounts were kept in Persian as well as Hindi, because by then the knowledge of Persian had become fairly widespread. This made the new language even more popular among the Hindus.

The break-up of the Delhi Sultanate (14th century) saw the establishment of several provincial dynasties which flourished until their reconquest by the Mughul Empire (17th century). Even when the Empire was strong, certain provincial governments, in recognition of the different traditions and geographical features of outlying areas, were given greater power and they encouraged local cultures. The first patrons, for instance, of the Bengali language and literature were the Muslim rulers of Bengal, and Bengali translations of even Hindu scriptures were dedicated to Muslim potentates. Perhaps the greatest contribution of the Muslims to the welfare of India was that they liberated the masses from the tyranny of Sanskrit classicism and encouraged the popular languages, hitherto considered vulgar. The results were naturally revolutionary and spectacular. Awakened into new life, the Hindus became eager to assimilate new ideas, and, under the patronage of the Mughuls, Muslim manners, idioms, ideas and etiquette became fashionable.

This gave the Muslims added confidence in the excellence of their culture and fortified them further in their own idealism.

Actually, the influence of Islam on Hindu culture was so great that only towards the end of the 19th century did the tide begin to turn. It was then that the Indian Muslim who, by constant endeavour, had tried to forge bonds of unity felt the first premonitions of their dissolution. He had held to the essentials of Islamic culture and was tenaciously loyal to the demands of his faith, but in other spheres he had gone more than halfway to meet the Hindu. He had almost entirely discarded his notions of music and had fallen a victim to the charms of Hindu classical music. It is true that his notions survived in popular strains, but even these depended for ultimate sanction on the canons propounded by the Hindu masters. He had kept the forms and symbolism of his poetry; but had permitted Hindu subtlety to creep into its very spirit. His notions of architecture were broadly Muslim; but he had allowed native masons to introduce Hindu features and motifs into all his buildings, even into the niche of the mosque which he faced while praying. Indian influence had crept into Muslim dress, even into Muslim cuisine. The chilli and tamarind had surreptitiously entered Muslim kitchens and begun to tickle palates which had gradually been growing dead to the natural flavours of meats and vegetables. An essentially Islamic vocabulary consisting of Arabic, Persian and Turkish words had sought the help of Prakritic grammar to make its syntax intelligible to the people of India. The Muslim had sacrificed the much easier, simpler, more regular and logical forms of Persian verbs and prepositions to win the understanding of the Hindu. In doing all this, he had remained a Muslim; but he ceased to be an Arab, a Turk, a Persian, or an Afghan. He had become an Indian Muslim; he had developed his own individuality, he became

conscious of his own culture. In this culture he had come to look
upon the cultured sections of the Hindus as his partners. He had
made no compromise in the matter of his own religious beliefs; he
did not expect the Hindus to compromise their religious beliefs.
He understood Hindu orthodoxy; he tolerated Hindu insistence
on looking upon the Muslim as unclean, as one in whose company
he would not eat; for all this he bore no ill-will, because he believed
that a common political life and cultural outlook provided ample
scope for co-operation. He built up a tradition of toleration which
provides very few parallels in history. The Maratha, Rajput and
Sikh rebellions against Mughul rule shook the very foundations of the handiwork of generations who had built a structure
of goodwill, but they did not succeed in demolishing the noble
edifice.

However, when, with the emergence of the British rule, the
spell of Muslim domination was broken, the Muslim hugged the
memory of a glorious past but the Hindu naturally changed his
orientation. With the same zeal as he had shown for Muslim
culture, he took to Western education. Just as the impact of
Islam had resulted in some conversions, Christianity began to
win converts. Just as Islam had been responsible for the rise of
cults which sought to bring about compromise between the
religion of the conqueror and the faith of the conquered, there
arose, as the result of Christian influence, movements which tried
to reform Hinduism in the light of Christian thought. Orthodox
Hinduism replied by revivalism, and in its anxiety to shake off all
extraneous influence it did not distinguish between Muslim and
Christian. Indeed there seemed to be some reason for adopting
Western notions, because now they were considered to be progressive and fashionable, but what reason could prevent the
Hindu iconoclast from purging Hinduism of Muslim influence?
The history of Hinduism in the last century is a record of
revivalist movements which have turned the Hindu mind to the
ancient pre-Muslim glory of India. In song classicism was born
again and the *ghazal* and *qawwali* grew unpopular, though the
monstrosities of film songs were appreciated, which are travesties
of European swing music. In art, the painter turned to Ajanta
for inspiration, though the Mughuls had gone much farther
ahead. In architecture, the arch and the dome were discarded,

the trabeate forms of pre-Islam were revived. In language, the
Prakritic structure was kept, but words of Muslim origin were
eschewed. The Arabic script introduced by the Muslims was
discarded in favour of the Sanskritic Deva-Nagri. Thus the
bridges which the Muslims had taken several hundred years to
build were burnt and in their place was left the deep, dark gulf.

These happenings had their political repercussions, but their
cultural and social results were even more important, because
they were responsible for the political cleavage which ultimately
resulted in the emergence of Pakistan.

The Muslim, in his endeavour to evolve an Indo-Muslim
culture, had Indianized himself. The Indo-Muslim culture had
a definite entity, though it varied considerably in its intensity.
The core of this culture was Islam, and its outer fringe faded into
the surrounding world of Hinduism. Its domain can be compared
to a series of concentric circles, its intensity decreasing with the
increase of distance from the centre. The centre was Islam, the
distance should be interpreted as remoteness from Islamic feeling.
Yet if we let alone religious belief, this culture at one time held
sway in varying degrees over the whole of India. When the
Hindus, conscious of new opportunities, started movements to
revive pre-Muslim forms of culture, the Muslim was left alone.
He was isolated. Indo-Muslim culture was his creation; it was
now the very blood of his vital veins. In so far as he was
Indianized, he had become a distinct group in the world of Islam;
in so far as he was a Muslim, he was a distinct group in India.
He had his connection with two worlds—the world of Islam and
the world of India. With the world of Islam the relationship was
spiritual, which continues even to-day. With India his relations
were physical, political and cultural. The physical relationship
continued, because he still lived in India and because of the size
of his group he could not leave it. He lost political power in India,
the cultural ties with the Hindu were broken by Hindu revivalism.
The Indian Muslims thus emerged as a distinct cultural group,
isolated, without political or economic power, but with a record
of great historical achievements. They were weak, but they formed
one-fourth of the entire population of India.

It is in the nature of revivalism that its dreams of the future
are based on the memories of the past. The ideal of the Hindu

revivalist was the India of the pre-Muslim past; the future development, therefore, had to take place on strictly Hindu lines. In the picture of such a future, Indian Muslims or Indo-Muslim culture could find no place. They had, according to certain thinkers, to be absorbed, as Hinduism had absorbed many a people and cult before. Others believed in ignoring them altogether. The Muslims themselves showed every symptom of decay. They were disorganized and weak. Their economic power was negligible, because they had failed to adapt themselves to new conditions. Educationally they were backward; their own educational system had withered away because it no longer enjoyed the patronage of the State and they were too proud and too suspicious to take kindly to the new system in the beginning. They had lagged behind, and the distance went on increasing. Poverty, ignorance and backwardness grow unless checked; it was no one's concern to arrest the decay; the task was too great for the Muslims themselves. Their resistance, it seemed, would soon break down, their consciousness would disappear.

This might have proved true. It may even now prove true in India. In a hundred years, perhaps in a shorter time, the Muslim people may cease to exist in that country. But the majority of the Indian Muslims were not in a mood to accept absorption. They wanted to live. Therefore, they resisted all efforts to undermine their existence. To Hindu revivalism their response was to strengthen their bonds with the pristine Islamic sources of their culture. Their language to-day has a larger percentage of Persian and Arabic words; they are intolerant of social customs which are Hindu in origin. The Reformist movements in Islam naturally aimed at restoring the pristine purity of doctrine and practice. If the Hindu looked upon the pre-Muslim past as his golden age, the Muslim replied by idealizing the achievements of his ancestors in India. The tale of Muslim conquest, looked upon by the Hindus as the story of national humiliation, was the record of the glory of his forefathers to the Muslim. All this brought about an estrangement in the relations of the Muslims with the Hindus which made the Muslims conscious of being a separate entity. As such they developed a strong sense not only of possessing a different religion, but also of a different social system and culture. The Islamic elements of this system and culture, never weak, were strengthened by the change in the outlook of the Hindus which had been growing more pronounced during the last few decades. The fact that the Muslim people in India were a separate entity expressed itself more visibly in dress, in domestic and public architecture, in language, in poetry, in utensils of daily use and in customs and manners. As Muslim opinion became more articulate, it tended to emphasize this truth. Westernization did not check this process, because it did not affect the springs of group consciousness either of the Hindus or of the Muslims. It only accentuated the feeling by its emphasis on grouping humanity into nationalities. The Hindus found in the doctrine of Indian nationalism an opportunity to consolidate their position, because they hoped to hold all the resources of the state with the help of their numbers, economic strength and superior education. The Muslims discovered that they were a nation by themselves. Hindu revivalism left them in possession of all the distinctive characteristics of a separate nation.

To the student of sociology, this is a significant phenomenon, because it was inevitable. An ancient people like the Hindus could not permanently reconcile themselves to the superiority of a culture whose foundations rested upon ideas alien to their philosophy, and therefore their revolt was intelligible and logical. The reaction of the Muslims was equally rational. This only shows that without a fundamental unity in ideals and outlook on life and a strong group sense even centuries of education on the part of rulers, thinkers, poets and saints cannot forge bonds strong enough to bind peoples into a single entity.

The emergence of a separate culture could not but have political consequences. The Muslims in India started with demands for separate representation and safeguards, but they ultimately discovered their futility and developed the conviction that nothing short of political independence could guarantee their existence as a distinct entity. Fortunately there were well-defined geographical areas where they formed the majority. They demanded that these areas should form a separate country and their determination won them this cherished goal which to-day stands enshrined in Pakistan.

The Pakistanis believe that they have glorious traditions of culture which they can further enlarge and develop. They maintain that their history has demonstrated their innate love of tolerance and liberalism, and, therefore, in a world where these virtues are at a discount, it is their duty to re-emphasize them by practising them in their own lives and upholding them in the world. The balance and proportion combined with lofty idealism and sense of beauty which their architecture has embodied for the world to witness can yet make the nation the architect of a future which will bring peace and happiness to themselves and good cheer to those who come into contact with them. Their leaders are never tired of repeating their ambition of basing the life of the nation on the Islamic principles of the brotherhood of man, tolerance, democracy and social justice. The Pakistanis are overwhelmingly Muslims and it is but natural that their national life and ideals will be fashioned by the ideology of Islam. This does not mean that non-Muslim minorities will be persecuted or deprived of the opportunity to live their lives in accordance with their own ideals and ways of thought. They are treated as equal partners in the polity and enjoy the fullest freedom in all religious and cultural matters, having been given the widest scope for development in these spheres. Islam itself ordains tolerance and generosity to the non-Muslim citizens of a predominantly Muslim State. The non-Muslim minorities are given all opportunities to enrich the life of the nation by their contributions in every walk of life. Islamic culture has never been exclusive and, at every stage of its development, non-Muslim citizens have made lasting contributions. The same spirit guides the Pakistanis.

The insistence of the Pakistanis on the spiritual and ethical principles enunciated by Islam has led their detractors to say that Pakistan is a theocratic State. Nothing could be farther from the truth. A theocracy is generally understood to mean the intolerant rule of an ordained priesthood who rule in the name of God because they occupy a special position in their capacity as His ministers. Such a conception of government is foreign to the Pakistani nation and also to Islam, which does not tolerate any form of priesthood. The Government has non-Muslim ministers, officials and legislators who participate in all deliberations and activities on a basis of complete equality. The legal system of a people and the trends of its public life must necessarily be the product of its ideals and beliefs, but this is so in every country.

If theocracy is taken in its literal sense and considered to be the rule of God, then, to a believer, the entire universe is a theocracy; but if the term implies intolerance or the rule of a class of priests, such a form of government not only does not exist in Pakistan but is also impossible. If the accusers mean that the people of Pakistan believe in certain spiritual and ethical values, then the nation must plead guilty to the charge. The Pakistanis do believe that government cannot be successfully divorced from all ideals; they further hold that if the peoples of the world draw greater inspiration from the noble truths of their religious or moral philosophies, it will result in greater happiness to humanity; and they staunchly believe that the principles enunciated by Islam can bring peace, tolerance and charity to a world distraught with narrow selfishness, immoral competition and blind greed. The pursuit of these ideals does not make Pakistan a theocracy.

The ideal man from the point of view of the overwhelming majority of the Pakistani nation is, naturally, Muhammad, the Prophet of Islam. He lived in the full glare of history; he is not a mythical or mysterious figure. We find him living as a poor man, caring neither for comfort nor worldly greatness, in a land where human ignorance, licence and greed had reached indescribable depths. He practised what he preached. Guided by an overwhelming consciousness of God and His perfection, he, an untutored dweller of the desert, was instrumental in giving to the world the quintessence of religion, not a religion. Born on the eve of the dawn of a New Age, he gave us principles which, according to our deepest convictions, are capable of bringing solace to a world which has lost the art of a balanced life, which no longer knows how to bring harmony between the spirit and the flesh, between true idealism and material needs. If there be any disbelievers in the efficacy of the Prophet's message, let them see how he brought peace to a land where warring tribes had carried on vendettas since times immemorial and welded them into a nation which held aloft the torch of progress and knowledge for several centuries in a dark, ignorant and intolerant world. Let them study what great spiritual and moral transformation was brought about in the people of Arabia. To-day the world would do well to give some thought to that message, because it is ailing from the same disease as Arabia did when Muhammad was entrusted by Providence to make one of the biggest and most successful experiments in history in the reconstruction of society by the application of spiritual and ethical principles to the life of a depraved people. Khadijah, the spouse of the Prophet, who helped him through her great insight and sympathy in his great task, is the ideal woman; she recognized the Truth when she first saw it and grudged no sacrifice in her endeavour to help her husband to establish it.

This also shows what the Pakistanis consider their principal and characteristic contribution to the cultural heritage of humanity in the 20th century. They have emerged as a distinct independent nation too recently to be able to point out any great works of art undertaken and finished during the short span of less than seven years. They can, even to-day, enumerate poets, writers, scientists and craftsmen in their midst. Their great national heritage they share with the Muslims of the entire sub-continent with whom they have a common history. They can enumerate great poets, architects, painters, scholars and writers who adorn the pages of their history. In the recent past lived their great poet Iqbal, who created in them the urge for freedom and independent statehood. His philosophy is inspired by Islam; indeed he knows no patriotism but that of his Faith. Their great painter Chaghtai is still living, who has the gift of capturing beauty by a few simple lines; whose technique is derived from the traditions of Central Asian, Persian and Mughul artists and whose imagination gives shapes to the most subtle fancies of Muslim poets. His work embodies the beauty of Muslim ideals and brings to life faces which lie embedded in the memories and dreams of the nation's subconscious mind. It is, however, not in Art and Literature that the Pakistanis think that their main contribution to the culture of the world will be made in the 20th century, though they attach great importance to these aspects of human progress. They think that their real contribution will be their emphasis on the ethical and moral principles which alone can save civilization.

CHAPTER II

The Family

THE family still retains its pre-eminence in Pakistan as the strongest bond of association. This is the result of universally recognized ethical principles, mostly based on religion. The duties of an individual to the family are well-defined and enshrined in tradition. Natural sentiment, fortified by religious and ethical concepts, is the firm basis on which the strength of the family is founded.

The family in Pakistan is, without any exceptions, patriarchal. The father is the head of the family; the mother is only second to him in authority. As the result of personal equation, it does, however, happen in some instances that the mother becomes the more dominant member. Generally speaking, the family runs smoothly, tradition having assigned to its members well demarcated spheres of authority. The father is the breadwinner and the mother runs the home. This demarcation works for harmony. Other members are consulted regarding their convenience, and they also participate, by expressing their opinions, in fashioning the family policy. Normally the family occupies an independent homestead and forms a small economic unit of consumers, and, sometimes, even of producers. The latter is true of craftsmen who manufacture commodities on the basis of cottage industry, and also of peasants. The members of the family share the goods which its combined income purchases, and except in the sophisticated urban areas the individual hardly ever keeps money separately for his own use.

The family generally consists of the father, the mother and their children. When a daughter grows up and is married, she naturally goes away to live with her husband. When a son is married, the young couple stay a while with his parents, even though they may be in a position to set up a separate home immediately. Sometimes this separation may be delayed because of harmonious relations for several years, but generally it takes place after a year or two. The family also retains some old relations, a widowed aunt or sister, even sometimes a daughter and her children. The aged parents continue to live, very often with their youngest son, even when the latter becomes the virtual head of a family of his own by his position as the breadwinner. The average family seldom exceeds three adults and four children; but of course there are many exceptions. The birth rate is high; the population has been increasing rapidly and, therefore, sometimes the number of children is large. Islam allows restricted polygamy but the number of men who marry more than one wife is exceedingly small, the average of polygamous marriages being less than one in ten thousand. Polygamy occurs when the first wife has no issue; in such instances the husband marries another wife at the request or even insistence of the first. Sometimes the second marriage may be the result of a desperate love affair. Among some small minorities like the Christians, polygamy is not practised. Hinduism puts no restrictions on polygamy or polyandry, but in Pakistan the latter is virtually unknown and the former is fairly scarce among the Hindus as well. As polygamy presupposes comparative freedom from economic difficulties, it does not entail poverty. Among the peasants or craftsmen, a second wife may mean an additional worker. Among the less prosperous, the two wives may live together, not always without friction; but among the rich the two wives live in separate houses and maintain independent establishments. Each wife is, virtually, the cell around which the structure of the family is built, the husband being the common link between two units. In such instances he has separate apartments and visits each unit of the family in rotation. This very often succeeds in eliminating friction and heart-burning. If it does not exist from the very beginning, an understanding soon grows up between the two units. Sometimes an undercurrent of veiled hostility also persists. The institution of polygamy, because of its rarity, does not materially alter what has been said about the size of the average family in this paragraph. Where the two units live separately, each one should be considered to be a family; where the two live together, the size increases, but there are extremely rare instances where it would reach the dimensions of two families united into one.

The Hindus possess an institution which deserves special mention. ' The joint family '—as it is called—consists of the aged father, his grown-up sons and their families, all living together. Sometimes, even where the common ancestor is dead, the brothers who have their own sons and grandchildren, even great-grandchildren, live together. Sometimes they may even live separately and yet maintain the joint family, because the joint family is an entity, recognized by law, deriving income from ancestral property, selling and mortgaging it, adding to it by purchase, carrying on trade, entering into contracts and paying taxes. One member is recognized as the *Karta,* the manager, and he is appointed with the consent of the adult male members of the family. Sometimes the joint family may not possess any property and yet exist, because then it is run by funds contributed or pooled by the earning members. The essence of the joint family is the willingness to live together, because if a sub-unit decides to separate, it can do so without much difficulty. The terms of such separation are laid down by the deceased ancestor by means of a will, or by the head of the joint family, or, in case of a dispute, even by a competent court. More often they are the outcome of an agreement. The joint family has certain advantages which have contributed to its long life. It serves as an insurance against sickness, old age, unemployment and, even, lack of competence. Its disadvantages are equally obvious. It limits the liberty of the individual because he must subordinate personal interests to those of the joint family; it tends to create a sense of complacence in the backward; in certain extreme cases it even kills initiative and enterprise. Its worst consequence is the position of the young wife whose personality is crushed under the rule of the most senior lady of the family, who rules with an iron hand. The sufferings of the young wife lead to sadism in her old age. Under the stress of modern conditions, the joint family is showing signs of weakness, but it is still far from extinction. It is obvious that the joint family has its roots in the remote past where the patriarch kept his progeny together so long as he could, because the largeness of the group gave it obvious advantages. It is also closely connected with the Hindu caste system which

will be described in another chapter. The Muslims developed
their family system on entirely different lines, partly because their
traditions were developed in countries outside the Indo-Pakistan
sub-continent and partly because their law is based on the recognition of individual rights and duties. The joint family is not found
even in the Muslim tribal areas.

The home plays a most important part in the life of the nation.
It is the centre of a man's life; he takes almost all of his meals
at home. The institutions of clubs and restaurants are still limited
to the big cities and, even there, it is a very small proportion of
the population which spends its time in these institutions. In the
rural areas there is nothing corresponding to a restaurant or even
a ' pub '; for social purposes men gather in village *chaupals* where
they smoke their tobacco pipes and talk of their little difficulties
and pleasures. In winter, there is a fire around which people sit
and indulge in all kinds of gossip. The meals, however, are taken
at home and most of the time is spent with the family and, therefore, the ties of family life are strong.

The home wields an important influence in the education of
the child because it is here that he learns the fundamentals of his
traditions and inherits the moral concepts and philosophy handed
down from generation to generation. This is truer about rural
areas where the percentage of schoolgoing children is low and
their knowledge of their crafts or agriculture is mostly traditional.
So is their religious and moral philosophy. In the towns and the
cities the school plays a more important part, but it never replaces
the influence of the home. The British introduced a system of
education which was not only secular to the most extreme degree
but also non-moral. The Muslims had, before the introduction
of the western system of education, their own traditional system
and, with the loss of their political power, they were afraid of
losing their cultural entity and moral and religious traditions.
Therefore, in the beginning they were openly hostile to the new
system and, when this hostility was softened by time and necessity,
they recognized the value of the new education, but looked upon
it purely as an instrument of material advancement. For moral
and religious concepts they still depended upon their religion and
traditional wisdom which did not remain static because of the
new influences. Nevertheless, in its fundamentals the new con-

7.
AN ART STUDENT

8.
A PAKISTANI
GIRL DRESSED
FOR TENNIS

9.
A PUNJABI
VILLAGE GIRL

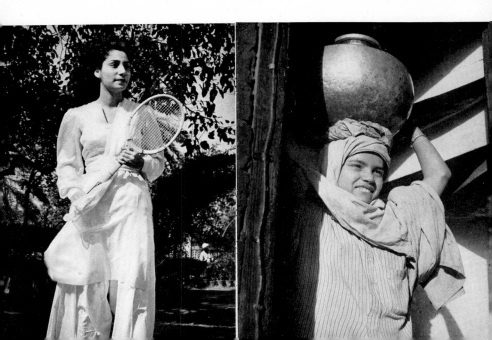

10. An Urban Family at Dinner

11. A Popular Tea Shop in the Suburbs of Karachi

sciousness was based upon traditions which were strong at home
and almost non-existent in the school. Pakistan is now evolving
a system where secular education may be tempered with Islamic
feelings and ideology, but this will take time. At present the
influence of the home continues to be the most potent factor in
fashioning the character of the average Pakistani Muslim. This
is true about the Pakistani Hindu as well. The Pakistani
Christians are in a different position. They are mostly educated
in schools run by missionaries, who make religious teaching an
integral and important part of their syllabus and, therefore, no
conflict arises between the influences of the home and the school
so far as they are concerned. This conflict will, it is hoped, cease
to exist for Muslims as well, because the educational system is
being given a new orientation.

The position of women differs from one religious group to
another. The Christian woman is emancipated in the Western
sense of the word and goes about her business just as any
European woman would, though even she has not reached the
same degree of sophistication as her Western sister. Her legal
rights are identical with those of her Christian sisters in the West
and politically she is on a par with her Muslim sisters in Pakistan.
The Muslim woman has very advanced legal rights. Whether
married or unmarried, she possesses property in her own right and
exercises all legal rights with respect to her possessions independently of her husband. She inherits property from her parents
and from other relations as well. As a daughter she inherits half
as much as a son does and she has definite shares in the inheritance from her other dead relations. She has political franchise
and there are women members of municipal corporations, provincial legislatures and the Federal Parliament.

Women are eligible for a large number of posts in the administration and lately they have been showing growing readiness
to bear the burden of their public responsibilities in an ever-
increasing degree. They are joining the nursing and medical
professions, becoming teachers, clerks, secretaries and are joining
the Women's National Guard. This, however, does not mean
that the women of Pakistan are as sophisticated as Western
women. Women in the villages work along with their menfolk
in the fields and do not wear the veil. In the towns and the cities

a larger proportion of the middle-class women are still behind the veil, though there is more literacy and even education in these classes. Among women who still wear the veil, one comes across women of culture and education. A small number, however, have discarded the veil and it is among these that most of the professional women are found, though all professional women have not necessarily discarded the veil. Among the non-professional women some who are highly educated have come out of the *pardah* (veil) and participate in social activities. The traditions of Islam enjoin a code of behaviour which is much more conservative than European ideas regarding the freedom of women. A new type of womanhood is, however, emerging in Pakistan which, at the present, tries to strike a balance between Islamic conservatism and European liberty by adhering to the moral code of Islam and adapting itself to the needs of the modern world. Whether they will succeed ultimately in doing so is yet to be seen.

The status of the Hindu woman is unfortunately less satisfactory. She has hardly any legal rights with reference to property. It is true that she is not behind the veil, but in most cases she very seldom leaves the precincts of her home. This, of course, does not apply to a small number of sophisticated Hindu women who attend social functions and are highly educated. In the average Hindu home the young wife is often the victim of the sadism of the older members of the family, and, in any case, is supposed to fag for the entire household. The plight of the young widow in a Hindu home is most miserable. Tradition enjoins that she should not participate in any pleasures or comforts. Her dress is coarse and simple and her food also is neither nourishing nor appetizing. When it is taken into consideration that religious prejudice and social customs do not permit even a child widow to re-marry, it will be understood what a cross she bears throughout her life.

Loyalty to the family seldom comes into conflict with patriotism on the emotional scale, but it would be wrong to say that in all cases the individual is able to rise above the narrow interests of his family in matters which affect his prosperity or advancement. Even then the love for the nation is strong and, when its implications are clearly understood, the mass of the people are willing to undergo suffering and make sacrifices. This has continuously been demonstrated by the refugees who have faced all kinds of difficulties most cheerfully.

Amongst the Muslims, patriotism involves loyalty to the country because there is no conflict between their group and national instincts. Inside the nation various groups have their local loyalties, as well as prejudices, which sometimes express themselves in elections or even in appointments to offices. But on a higher plane they are not permitted to come into conflict with the national feeling. As a peace-loving people the Pakistanis want a peaceful and harmonious world because they have no extra-territorial ambitions and only want to be left alone so that they may build up a happy and prosperous country.

CHAPTER III

Educational System

PAKISTAN covers some of the areas which have an ancient tradition of civilization and culture. The sites of the ancient cities of Mohenjo Daro and Harappa lie within its territories and thus this country can look back to continuous history of intellectual progress and achievement for many centuries. After the coming of the Aryans some of the Vedas were written in the Western Punjab, and in the days of Buddhism Takshashila—now known as Taxila—was an educational centre of international reputation. With the Arab conquest of Sind, the Muslim system of education was introduced in this area and a number of cities attained fame in the Islamic world for their intellectual activity. Of these Mansura, Sehwan, Thatta and Multan are well known. When the Ghaznawids conquered the West Punjab, Lahore became a centre of learning and culture. Thatta, Multan and Lahore maintained their traditions throughout the period of Muslim rule. In the east Gaur, and then Dacca, attained the same eminence.

The Muslim system of education provided a happy blending of secular and religious learning. This was possible because of the rational approach of Islam towards life. The Quran appeals neither to superstition nor to abstruse speculation; on the contrary, it again and again lays emphasis on the rational faculty of man and his observation of Nature. The sturdy commonsense of the Arab, as is well known, laid the foundation of an enlightened philosophy and created an attitude of mind which did not eschew knowledge. The Arabs were great learners and teachers. Their great achievement was the result of their ability to assimilate all that was best in the learning of the civilized world at that time. Having assimilated this vast store of human knowledge and experience, they improved upon it and then spread it into every nook and corner of their empire. Sind, therefore, was the inheritor of this great awakening. The House of Ghaznih was known for its patronage of learning and culture; it founded traditions at Lahore which later spread to all the corners of the sub-continent along with the Muslim rule. The Mughul Empire inherited the traditions of the earlier Muslim dynasties and passed them on to the entire Muslim people of this sub-continent.

It would be useful to give some description of the method of education which prevailed in Muslim India. Education was not controlled by the State, though it was one of the greatest patrons of learning and education. The State subsidized education by founding universities and colleges and granting scholarships and stipends to deserving teachers and students. Every college was a pious foundation and the God-fearing always considered it their duty to endow places of learning generously, even lavishly. These institutions charged no fees and the students who flocked to their portals were maintained throughout their career by colleges. They were given free board and lodging and were supplied with books without cost. Education was thus free and anyone who felt interested could obtain it. The attainment of knowledge and its dispensation were alike regarded as acts of worship and there grew up a tradition in accordance with which even the wealthy and powerful found a little time to teach such as desired knowledge. After the decline of their power the Muslims were left in possession of large endowments for educational purposes, but they gradually lost most of them, because, in many places, the British took over these foundations and spent the money on objects not covered by the terms of the endowments. Muslim education thus starved.

The subjects taught in the old Muslim schools and colleges were the Muslim classics of Arabic and Persian, Theology, History, Philosophy, Logic, Astronomy, Physics, Chemistry, Medicine, Mathematics, Mechanical and allied Sciences. The educational system was firmly based upon the idealism of Islam, but the human mind was not fettered in its search for truth by any cramping influence of authority. This system also bred its sceptics and rebels, though the atmosphere of the college and the school was not conducive to the development of an irreligious bent of mind. Its distinctive advantage was that it was in harmony with the idealism of the community and there was no conflict between moral concepts and the subject matter of the teaching.

With the introduction of the Western system of education by the British all this was changed. Macaulay, who conceived the idea of introducing Western education into the Indo-Pakistan sub-continent, was guided by conflicting notions. He unjustly and ignorantly said that a single book of English was worth libraries of oriental learning—a statement which could be made only by one whose vision was narrow and whose knowledge of the subject meagre. This contempt for oriental learning and hostility towards it led him to lay the foundation of a system which had no relation to the traditions of the culture which he sought to destroy. His idea was frankly to create an army of clerks and petty admini-strators who would understand the language of the British rulers and carry out their orders. This was the immediate target; the ultimate object was the impossible task of creating a race of brown Englishmen. Macaulay's successors did succeed in achiev-ing his first target, but Nature would not let them achieve the ultimate object of the creation of a new nation of Englishmen with some pigment in their skins. Just as it would be impossible to remove the pigment even if an endeavour were made, it was difficult to uproot the entire strata of tradition and moral con-cepts which contributed to the mental equipment of the people.

Actually the British educationists who ran the educational system in this sub-continent never seriously undertook the task of creating a new nation. They limited themselves to creating a class of petty officials who might help the administration. They also tried, at least in the beginning, to bring about a rebellion against the older traditions of culture, religion and ideology, but they seldom devoted themselves to the creation of the traditions of scholarship and research. When the universities had existed for several decades and a large number of natives went to Europe for education, they brought back from the European universities certain ideas and traditions and gradually a respect for standards, research and scholarship began to emerge. The position in Pakistan, therefore, is that there exist side by side two educational systems. The older Islamic system of education has been, for lack of patronage, in a state of decadence. It is almost dying; but the values for which it stood are still recognized and command loyalty.

12. A Labourers' Village in the Suburbs of Karachi

13. A Fruit Vendor's Shop in Peshawar

14. SCHOOL CHILDREN AT EXERCISE

15. STUDENTS OF BOTANY IN THEIR CLASSROOM

The Western system of education has improved because of the later contribution of Pakistani scholars and teachers. But it is now widely recognized that Pakistan requires a new educational system which may bring about a reconciliation between secular and religious knowledge and which may create traditions of scholarship and research impregnated with the ideology of Islam. At the present time the Pakistani nation is trying to create a system of education which may be deeply rooted in her past and yet not be out of tune with the present world. In this way it is the endeavour of her educationists to build up a future for the nation in consonance with the dictates of History and progress.

The present educational structure may now be described. After the pre-primary or infant stage a child remains at school for ten years, when he matriculates. During this time he is taught Urdu, English, a classical language (Persian, Arabic, Sanskrit or Latin), Mathematics, History, Geography and elements of Science. He is about fifteen years old when he matriculates. Then he goes to the university. He graduates in four years and then, if he desires to pursue post-graduate studies, he takes the Master's Degree in another two years. If he so desires, he can study for a Doctorate after taking his Master's Degree. The length of the professional courses varies; so do the academic requirements of admission. The school education is divided into primary and secondary stages. Naturally the largest number of students are to be found in the primary schools. The number of pupils who go up for secondary education is much smaller. The proportion, however, of those who go to a university after their matriculation is, comparatively speaking, higher. At the school stage a pupil has to pass either an informal admission examination before being admitted or produce a certificate of having attended another school and achieved a standard or both. Public examinations at present are the High School or Matriculation Examination and in the university the Intermediate Examination and then the various Diploma and Degree Examinations. No student can be admitted for a Degree unless he has passed the previous examinations, pursued a regular course of studies and then taken the examination leading to the particular degree. The condition of having pursued a regular course of studies is relaxed under certain conditions.

Schoolmasters are recruited from amongst persons who have been trained in pedagogy. There are normal schools to train teachers for the primary classes, training schools for teachers with lower qualifications and training colleges for teachers with higher qualifications. At the university stage teachers are recruited from amongst the more brilliant graduates who ultimately, on the basis of their scholarship and research, may rise to occupy university chairs. The educational standards required of university and college teachers are high and it is generally recognized that the quality of the university depends upon the attainments of its teachers.

At the primary stage and also in the universities co-education is fairly common. At the secondary stage it does not exist and is discouraged. In the universities, whereas lectures are common for men and women, the residential units are always separate and unrestricted mixing of sexes is not encouraged either by society or by the authorities. In schools, particularly when the children are young, some technical education forms part of their syllabus, but at later stages it ceases to be compulsory. In the universities, science is becoming more and more popular, and emphasis is being laid upon the foundation of faculties and institutions of technical training to an extent that there is some danger of the humanities being neglected in the near future, but hitherto more students have taken to the humanities than to sciences. This is partly the result of the shortage of laboratories and the restricted means at the disposal of institutions. There is a keen competition for entrance into medical and technical institutions and even the science departments of colleges and schools tend to be overcrowded and a large number of applicants have to take up humanities because there is no room for them in science. Philosophy is taught purely from the objective point of view and hitherto the Western philosophers and their writings form the main theme of lectures and studies. Occasionally some place is given to oriental and Islamic philosophy. Ethics also is taught as a branch of philosophy and it is divorced from the teachings of any particular religion. Civics forms part of the curricula in schools and the early stages of university education. The education given in the universities is secular. Only recently Islamic theology has been introduced as a subject of study for Muslim students. There are separate seminaries and institutions for religious education which still follow all the Muslim traditions. These institutions are dependent on private philanthropy. They are exceedingly conservative and their system of teaching is authoritarian.

Education in the universities, however, is liberal and no shackles are put upon human thought. The universities are autonomous bodies incorporated by various Acts of Legislatures. There is, however, a certain amount of Government control so far as their management is concerned, because the Government gives them liberal grants and is, therefore, represented on their administrative bodies. The representation of the Government, however, is not large and the main power accrues to it from the fact that the universities would find it difficult even to exist without its financial aid. There is very little actual interference by the Government and the universities have almost complete authority. They are completely free from any political influence from the Government.

The universities are mostly secular in character and, because they are practically free from Government control, both the teachers and the pupils have free scope for fashioning their thought on the lines that they desire and, naturally, there is considerable amount of debating, criticism and interchange of thought. The seminars, the debating clubs, the class-room and the research departments all contribute to the development of the critical faculty of the pupils.

The relations between the teachers and the pupils vary from institution to institution. The smaller institutions, where the proportion of pupils to the number of teachers is smaller, have a healthier tradition of close contacts between the teachers and the pupils. In larger institutions, where the number of teachers is smaller, this close relationship is difficult to cultivate. In schools, teachers take considerable part in extra-mural activities of the students; at the university stage the participation of teachers in these activities continues though its nature changes. In the university the student is more mature and he generally likes to be independent, though his relations with his teachers remain friendly and sometimes even intimate. There is a very long tradition in all oriental countries of respect for the teachers. This, for reasons enumerated later, has considerably diminished, but it still persists. When a teacher has some eminence as a scholar, or if his character inspires respect, he generally succeeds in winning the loyalty and affection of his pupils. As the result of the tradition of a political struggle where the students could not be effectively prevented from indulging in political activities against the British rule and the teachers were subject to a more rigorous discipline, the hold of the teachers on their pupils grew weaker. One of the reasons was that strikes and demonstrations by students were political instruments of some potency and, therefore, political leaders made use of them. The teacher, on the other hand, had an academic outlook and liked the student to remain in the class-room rather than become a political worker. Besides, there was conflict of loyalties between those who were advocates of Pakistan and those who opposed it. Throughout the sub-continent, before the transfer of the population, most of the institutions were mixed and had a proportion of Hindu and Muslim pupils and teachers. The political cleavage had its repercussions upon educational institutions as well, and relations with the teachers were often determined by political affiliations. These difficulties have now been removed but still there are certain vague traces of the lack of confidence in the teacher visible in some institutions where the student does not look upon the teacher as his natural friend, philosopher and guide. This tendency, however, is diminishing because of the fervour of a common ideology.

The relations amongst the pupils themselves are now normal and friendly. Before the Partition the political cleavage between the Hindus and the Muslims made itself felt in the educational institutions as well. In Western Pakistan, where the number of non-Muslims is very meagre, the problem has completely disappeared and student life is once again without the harmful influence of political rancour or cleavage. In Eastern Pakistan the friendly atmosphere of student life has been restored. Students are organized into various clubs and societies in their several universities and institutions for academic and social purposes or for games and sports. There are also several all-Pakistan bodies of students which have their contacts with other student bodies of the world.

Freedom has brought in its wake a new enthusiasm for education and, therefore, in spite of the multiplication of schools, colleges and universities, all institutions are overcrowded. As soon as a new institution comes into existence students rush to it for admission. There were only two universities in the beginning, which were functioning indifferently; to-day there are six; but each one of these six is so overcrowded that discipline and standards have alike been affected adversely. For instance, the tribesmen in the North-West Frontier Province in the days of the British rule considered a school to be an instrument of imperialist expansion. Therefore, they resisted all attempts to establish schools in their territories. They had to be threatened, cajoled or bribed into accepting a school. Even when accepted the school was thinly attended. To-day the tribesmen desire nothing more than the expansion of educational facilities in their areas. A large number of schools have been opened and they still demand more. It had been customary for the Governor of the North-West Frontier Province to distribute small sums of money to children for purchasing sweets when he visited a tribal village. Recently, when the Governor went to a village and he offered a rupee to a small girl of nine years she refused to accept it and demanded instead that the primary school in her village should be raised to the secondary standard. The demand for the expansion of educational facilities throughout Pakistan is so great that the best efforts of the Government are not able to keep pace with the demand. A country which has so recently started developing its industry and expanding its economy does not find it easy to find all the financial resources for such a rapid expansion of its educational system; but this is not the only problem. It is not easy to train teachers in sufficiently large numbers and sometimes untrained teachers have to be employed. Education has hitherto tended to be mostly theoretical. The number of technical and vocational institutions is small. Industrial development has created a demand for technical personnel which is difficult to meet. Therefore new technical institutions are being established. Here again the difficulties in finding the necessary money and personnel are almost overwhelming. The shortage of institutions has resulted in overcrowding, which has adversely affected standards and discipline. When a teacher has to deal with too large a number of pupils, he cannot devote the same attention to their individual progress, nor can he exercise his beneficial influence upon their character and sense of discipline. A long tradition of resistance to authority under foreign domination and participation in politics is not easy to eradicate and contributes to indiscipline among students. It is hoped that these tendencies will disappear with increasing facilities for education and healthy student activities.

The contacts between teachers and parents have yet to be developed properly. Only a few schools have occasional gatherings of teachers and parents, and the movement has not registered much progress.

Apart from the education in schools and colleges, the Government has sponsored various movements for adult education and education of the working classes. The most significant of these is the Village A.I.D.* Programme which aims at creating in the villager a desire for improving his living conditions by self-help through fundamental education. Various centres for training workers to carry out this programme have been opened throughout the country and teams have been sent abroad to be trained in the U.N.E.S.C.O. programme of fundamental education. A team of experts has been working in the vicinity of Karachi and the results achieved are encouraging. In certain areas which are thinly populated the villages are at considerable distance from one another and some of them are merely clusters of three or four families living sometimes at a distance of thirty to forty miles away from any inhabited area. It is difficult to cater for them. An experiment, however, has been made by creating units of mobile schools. The teacher takes a truck to the village and, in the shade of an awning or even a tree, he collects adults and children alike and gives them lessons twice or thrice a week. This programme is still in the experimental stage, but the results achieved are fairly promising. So far as the working classes are concerned, they are better off because they are concentrated in compact areas and it is easier for teachers and social workers to reach them. A number of larger mills and factories also provide facilities for adult education to their workers.

In the other spheres of education the most prominent part is played by the political activities of the various organizations. For the achievement of Pakistan intensive propaganda had to be

* A = Agricultural ; I = Industrial ; D = Development.

carried out amongst the Muslim population which resulted in considerable political awakening. Not a hamlet was without its political organizer and not a home remained which did not receive and respond to the message of Pakistan. The implications of the Partition and its necessity were broadcast by political workers and understood by the nation at large. The interest thus created in political activity has survived because of the dangers inherent in the life of the new country, and the people have developed considerable political consciousness. This leads them to try to understand the various policies and measures of the Government and, if they disagree, they express their views cogently and emphatically. They are also conscious of the world conditions which have a bearing upon their lives. The policies of the various big powers and groups, the part played by the United Nations and, in particular, the trends in the neighbouring country of India are the subject of conversation. Freedom is so new to the people of Pakistan that they have not lost interest in it and, therefore, in their desire to preserve it, they want to gain a fuller understanding of their difficulties and the environment in which they have to live. This political consciousness is not without its drawbacks. The desire for progress sometimes creates impatience and even frustration, which combined with inexperience in working democratic institutions gives an opportunity to irresponsible demagogues and subversive agitators, as some events have recently shown.

The Radio is owned by the State and along with entertainment provides instruction which takes the form of talks on a large variety of subjects. A number of instructive feature programmes and plays are broadcast and, without reducing the entertainment value of broadcasting, the State follows an enlightened policy of imparting education. The radio broadcasts special programmes for school-children and university students. Women's programmes also are a regular feature and the news broadcasts devote considerable time to the happenings in the world. Art, poetry, films, short stories and literary articles are vehicles of education. Similarly the periodicals published by various institutions and private organizations are popular. The film industry plays its part, though here mostly entertainment is the main aim. The Government produces documentaries for the purposes of mass education and practically every provincial and state government has at its disposal several units of mobile cinema vans which go to the villages for publicity.

Pakistan has a fairly strong Press. Six dailies and some weeklies are published in the English language which command a good circulation. Even more powerful, however, is the vernacular Press. A large number of dailies and weeklies are published in various parts of the country, the dailies alone numbering more than two dozen. Some of these papers have built up large circulations and are powerful media of education and expression of opinion. The more sober papers are excellent means of education because they comment upon national and international affairs with objectivity and restraint and publish a large number of articles and reports from special correspondents upon the happenings of the world and the problems which face different countries at different times. Like every country Pakistan also has its counterpart of the sensational press of which the educational value is doubtful.

Games and sports are popular. Apart from some of the indigenous traditional sports which find favour in the villages, European sports are also becoming popular. Pakistan maintains an excellent standard in hockey, association football and polo. Cricket and tennis have a large number of votaries and there would hardly be a place where volley ball is not played, because it is one of the cheapest forms of exercise and amusement. Recently, basket-ball has been gaining popularity. There is a long tradition of wrestling; a Pakistani wrestler is the world champion. Similarly in squash rackets, Pakistani players have remained unbeaten. The Council for Physical Education, Pakistan Olympic Association with its subsidiary bodies, the Board of Control for Cricket and federations for various games are responsible for maintaining standards and providing encouragement. The Government subsidizes these bodies.

CHAPTER IV

Political Institutions and Aspirations

It has already been mentioned that the traditions of civilization in Pakistan go far back into antiquity. The excavations at Mohenjo Daro, Harappa and Taxila have revealed a stage in development where municipal organization must have become fairly complex and efficient. In the sub-continent of India, as elsewhere, the development in the towns and the rural areas was more or less on parallel lines. The complexity of the organization of the town could not be expected in the structure of the village, but the sub-continent has a long tradition of comparative self-sufficiency in the village. This made the organization of village government also necessary. As these town and village communities were scattered over large stretches of land, often separated from one another by dense forests or other barriers, they necessarily became comparatively self-sufficient and self-governing. The empires which rose and fell before the establishment of Muslim rule should be envisaged more as federations of small self-governing communities paying homage and taxes to a central authority rather than well-knit entities having strong centralized governments. At a very early stage during the period of Rajput domination, the structure of government became feudal in character. This was necessary because of the difficulties of communication and the nature of economic and tribal organization. Under the Rajputs, therefore, we find that the village as well as the town maintained its comparative self-sufficiency as well as some measure of self-government. As the result of military exigencies, however, they became subservient to local chieftains who rendered such homage as they considered necessary to the authority at the centre.

The Muslims had developed a bureaucratic system before they entered India. Their government was more highly centralized

and depended for its efficiency upon public servants who were
paid either salaries in cash or whose salaries were, for the sake
of convenience, commuted into assignments of State revenues in
certain areas. Their system of government was different from
feudalism in two essential features. Its first characteristic was that
the public servants had no hereditary interest in the position they
occupied or the service to which they belonged unless, of course,
their association created a predilection in the minds of their
children for that particular service. In such instances they had
to seek entry purely on merits and then to work their way up in
accordance with their talent and capacity. The other difference
was that these public servants were transferable from one place to
another. Their assignments were assumed or transferred in accordance with convenience and when they died they lost all interest
in the assignment. Naturally, the assignment was increased or
decreased in accordance with promotion or demotion.

Throughout the period of Muslim rule in India we find the
government a well-organized and efficient bureaucracy guided
by enlightened principles of public service and benevolence, which
were enunciated by jurists and writers on public administration.
The Muslim rule was certainly despotic, but it was an enlightened
and benevolent despotism. Their system of agrarian administration was deep-rooted in the traditions of the soil which were
fundamentally in agreement with their own experience in adjoin-
ing lands and notions based on their religion. Their system of
administration of justice was scientific and the law that they
administered had been developed by jurists and lawyers of considerable erudition and acumen. They were fully aware of the
Roman principles of jurisprudence. In evolving their system of
jurisprudence they had taken account of the principles developed
in different countries and had adapted them to the tenets of their
religion. They had thus produced a legal system which was far
ahead of other contemporary systems. Under Muslim rule, the
insistence upon and organization for social services was most
remarkable. Therefore, when the British came into the sub-
continent, in spite of the fact that government had broken down
as the result of widespread anarchy and the rise of turbulent
chieftains and communities, the principles of administration which
the Muslims had popularized in the sub-continent were still

16.
KARACHI:
THE BUSINESS
CENTRE, WITH
THE MUNICIPAL
CORPORATION
BUILDING

17.
A PART OF
THE PUNJAB
UNIVERSITY

19. Fishing in Eastern Pakistan

18. A Bargain Amongst the Pathans.
Young Lambs have just Changed Hands

widely accepted as essential for good government and the art of administration had not completely died out. As a matter of fact the British built upon these foundations. In certain spheres they departed from the old principles only to injure their benevolent character. For instance, in the sphere of agrarian administration, for a system based upon peasant proprietorship, they introduced a form of landlordism which had no redeeming features.

The traditions of bureaucracy which had already existed were further polished and improved by the British and by the end of the last century administration had been put on a sound basis. By the beginning of the First World War the machine had begun to function smoothly and fairly efficiently. There was no deterioration in the organization of the administration between the two World Wars. But the hold of the British on the sub-continent was considerably weakened by the rise of popular feeling for self-government and independence. During the period of the last World War, the efficiency of the administrative machinery suffered considerably; corruption, which had never been completely wiped out, once again received impetus. To-day the administrative organization is the same as was modelled by the British; it has not been changed to any considerable degree. There is, however, a complete change in the personnel as well as the spirit of the administration. Nationalization of services had started soon after 1918; its speed had been considerably accelerated during the period of the last World War. To-day the services in Pakistan are almost entirely manned by her own nationals, but there are a few public servants of British origin who have not chosen to retire because of the change in the government. Their number is very small and, as they retire, they are being replaced by Pakistani officials.

The political organization of Pakistan also has a history. When the British took over the administration of these areas they established a system of government which was not responsible to the people. With the pressure of public opinion, however, elected representatives of the people were taken into the legislatures as early as the beginning of this century (1909) and with the introduction of the Government of India Act, 1919, the popular element in the provincial and central legislatures increased considerably. The Government of India Act, 1935, established full provincial autonomy and envisaged self-government at the centre with certain safeguards to maintain the control of Great Britain over the central government. The part of the Act which concerned the provinces was made operative in 1937. But there was unanimous opposition to the enforcement of such portions of the Act as related to the central government. The pressure of the demand for independence resulted in a series of conferences and attempts at compromise, but ultimately in the year 1947 it was decided to set up two independent sovereign Dominions of Pakistan and India.

For this purpose, the British Parliament enacted the Independence Act of 1947. It set up separate constituent assemblies for India and Pakistan. The Constituent Assembly was empowered to enact a constitution for the country; pending the enactment of the new constitution, Pakistan was governed under the Independence Act of 1947 and the Government of India Act 1935, as adapted by the Constituent Assembly of Pakistan. The original Act was an Act of the British Parliament. Under this arrangement, the Queen of the United Kingdom was the Queen of Pakistan. Her main functions were the appointment of the Governor-General and the accrediting of Pakistani ambassadors; both of these functions were discharged by the monarch on the advice of her Pakistani ministers. The Governor-General, like the Queen, was expected to be a constitutional head; the real power was to be exercised by a cabinet responsible to the Constituent Assembly, which was to act as the national parliament pending the enforcement of a new constitution. The government was to be federal; the federating units were the provinces of East Bengal, West Punjab, Sind, the North-West Frontier Province and Baluchistan and such princely states as acceded to the Federation. Of these the more important were Bahawalpur, Khairpur, Kalat, Las Bela, Makran, Chitral, Swat and Dir. The tribal territories in the north-west also acceded through their representative assemblies, the *jirgahs*. Karachi was taken out of the province of Sind and constituted into a separate administrative unit as the federal capital in 1948. The offices of the federal government were located at Karachi from the beginning; the decision of the Constituent Assembly to make it the capital came a little later. All the provinces except Baluchistan and the federal capital had their own legislatures and cabinets of ministers under governors appointed by the federal government. Baluchistan was administered by an officer appointed by the federal government and known as the Agent to the Governor-General. The princely states were autocracies, all powers being exercised by the ruler. Under the British these states had varying degrees of autonomy; foreign relations, defence and communications were invariably under the paramount power. These states under their first instruments of accession surrendered these three subjects to the federation. Subsequently, however, most of the states executed supplementary instruments, either surrendering further powers or accepting the principle of democratic administration; in this way democratic institutions of responsible government were created in several states; the more advanced like Bahawalpur and Khairpur became constitutional monarchies with such powers as had not been surrendered to the federation being in practical effect vested in their legislatures and cabinets responsible to them. The princes exercised only such constitutional powers as the summoning of the legislature or the formal appointment of the leader of the majority as the chief minister. Where the establishment of full responsible government was not considered feasible, steps were taken to associate the people increasingly with the administration as an interim measure.

The Constituent Assembly was confronted with grave problems. The geographical peculiarity of a country existing in two regions with a thousand miles of foreign and unfriendly territory separating the two posed problems which required circumspection. In the first flush of enthusiasm the Assembly treated East Bengal as just any other province in spite of the fact that, though it covers only about 16 per cent. of the territory, it contains nearly 56 per cent. of the population. Besides, the attachment to the regional language was too strong to make it feasible for the Bengalis to accept a single national language for the entire country. East Bengal also faced greater economic maladjustment in the wake of the Partition, because its port of outlet, Calcutta, had gone to India and it took some time to put Chittagong in shape for dealing with the overseas trade of this region, which also includes the trade with Western Pakistan. Such troubles caused grievances against the party in power. Provincial elections in East Bengal, held on the basis of adult franchise in March 1954, made this amply clear, when the Muslim League Party was swept away in a landslide victory for the opposition groups combined under the United Front. It became obvious that East Bengal would not accept a constitution framed by the old Constituent Assembly.

This was not the only difficulty confronting the First Constituent Assembly. As has been mentioned earlier, Western Pakistan was a conglomeration of self-governing provinces, princely states in various stages of political development, areas administered on a tribal basis and areas anxious to have a responsible form of government, but economically too poor or under-developed to be able to sustain the paraphernalia of legislative assemblies, cabinets and secretariats. Should they respect the existing boundaries, even though they did not represent or correspond to ethnical or linguistic divisions? How far should regional patriotism be taken into account?

Another problem was to translate Islamic feelings and ideals into constitutional forms. The constitution makers did not want to divide the nation into two camps of traditionalists and modernists; they themselves did not believe in throwing traditions and idealism overboard; nor did they want to discard the modern patterns of democracy, because they believed that they were in accord with their own aspirations and the true spirit of Islam. The discussion of such problems raised controversy and differences of opinion. Several suggestions were openly mooted and discussed and public reactions summarized and circulated. All this took time and no solution arose which did not have obvious drawbacks.

In spite of these difficulties, the First Constituent Assembly did succeed in agreeing upon the basic principles and a draft constitution was ready. It was intended to enact it finally before December 25, 1954. The Governor-General, however, dissolved the Assembly in October, and, therefore, its work remained unfinished. It, however, had done all the basic work; it was the record of its deliberations and findings which made it possible for the Second Constituent Assembly to produce a constitution within such a short period. The political and legal consequences of the dissolution of the First Constituent Assembly will find a brief mention elsewhere; here it will suffice to say that a new Assembly was elected in 1955 and applied itself to the writing of a constitution. It finished its work in time for the constitution to be enforced on March 23, 1956.

The constitution of Pakistan is a detailed and lengthy document. It is divided into thirteen parts containing 234 articles; in addition there are six schedules. It is further sub-divided into the operative part of the constitution, which is justiciable and can be enforced by the courts of law, and the directive principles of state policy, which embody the aspirations and the desires of the framers of the constitution without any binding authority. This part has only nine articles, so that the operative part is the major portion of the constitution. The constitution is rigid; it can be amended by an Act of Parliament ' if a bill for that purpose is passed by a majority of the National Assembly, and by the votes of not less than two-thirds of the members of that Assembly present and voting, and is assented to by the President '; however, certain clauses can be amended only if the provincial legislatures endorse the amendment. In the latter category are the clauses mostly dealing with the interests of the provinces, like their jurisdiction and representation in the federal parliament. All the provinces and areas formerly situated inside Western Pakistan including the princely states have been constituted into the single province of West Pakistan. The only exception is the area of the federal capital, Karachi, which is under the federal government directly. Such tribal areas as have not been fully integrated have still their former institutions of government; but now the entire territory is represented in the provincial legislature. Thus Pakistan now consists of two provinces —West Pakistan and East Pakistan—and the federal capital. Each of the two provinces has a unicameral legislature consisting of 300 members. The governor is appointed by the federal government; he is the constitutional head of the provincial government; the real power is vested in a cabinet of ministers who are severally and jointly responsible to the provincial Assembly.

At the federal level, the head of the State is the President, who is elected by ' an electoral college consisting of the members of the National Assembly and the Provincial Assemblies.' He must be a Muslim, at least forty years old, and qualified for election as a member of the National Assembly. He holds office for five years and can serve for a maximum of two terms. He can be removed by impeachment on a charge of violating the constitution or gross misconduct. In cases of his absence from the country or illness, the Speaker of the National Assembly acts as the President. The constitution lays it down that the President's executive authority shall be exercised ' in accordance with the advice of the Cabinet or the appropriate minister '; the exceptions to this are the appointment of the Public Service Commission and the Election Commission. The real power is vested in a cabinet of ministers who are severally and jointly responsible to the National Assembly. The Parliament consists of the President, who is not a member of the National Assembly, and the National Assembly, which has a membership of 300 members, 150 each from East Pakistan and Western Pakistan. All legislators, whether provincial or federal, are elected on the basis of adult franchise. The National Assembly can be summoned, prorogued or dissolved by the President on the advice of the Prime Minister. A provincial Assembly can be likewise summoned, prorogued or dissolved by the provincial governor on the advice of the chief minister of the province. Unless sooner dissolved the life of each of these assemblies is five years from the date of its first meeting.

The constitution provides for an independent judiciary. The Supreme Court is the final court of appeal in the country; it has also the powers of interpreting the constitution. Each province has its own High Court, which, in addition to appellate functions and supervisory authority over the subordinate courts, has the power to issue writs in the nature of *habeas corpus, mandamus*, prohibition, *quo warranto* and *certiorari* for the enforcement of the fundamental rights defined in the constitution. There are twenty articles in the part which deals with fundamental rights; they guarantee freedom of speech, association, assembly, movement, trade, business, profession and religion; equality before law and protection against retrospective offences and punishments. They prohibit slavery and forced labour, untouchability, discrimination in services or access to public places; they safeguard preservation of culture, script and language and a number of other rights.

The areas of the jurisdiction of the federal and provincial authority have been defined by drawing up three lists of subjects, federal, provincial and concurrent. The first contains defence, foreign affairs, immigration, citizenship, foreign trade and commerce, currency, coinage, foreign exchange, copyright, patents, mineral oil and natural gas, census and a few subsidiary matters. Economic and social planning, iron, coal, steel and mineral products other than oil and natural gas, scientific and industrial research and a few other matters are on the concurrent list. What does not appear on these lists is by inference on the provincial list because the provinces have been given residuary powers, though a list of provincial subjects is appended. In the concurrent field, the Acts of the federal Parliament supersede provincial measures irrespective of the time sequence.

The official name of the country according to the constitution is the Islamic Republic of Pakistan, though the shorter Pakistan is permitted. This brings us to the Islamic provisions in the constitution. Apart from the name of the Republic and the provision that the President shall be a Muslim, there are two articles specifically devoted to this question. The first provides for setting up an organization for Islamic research and instruction in advanced studies to be financed entirely out of funds raised by taxing Muslims alone. The second provides for a commission to be set up by the President to report in five years how the laws of the land can be brought into conformity with the fundamental teachings of Islam and to draw up in a suitable form such injunctions of Islam as can be given legislative effect; after they have been accepted by the Parliament no law shall be enacted which is repugnant to them. It has been clearly laid down that this shall not refer to the personal law of the non-Muslim minorities and, in case of different schools of thought in Islam, shall be interpreted in accordance with their accepted views in the matter. Except in the appointment of the President, no discrimination is permitted against any religious or racial minority.

The fact that Pakistan has been declared to be a Republic shows that the Queen of the United Kingdom has no legal or political jurisdiction in the country. She is recognized solely as the symbolic head of the Commonwealth.

This brings us to the question of the membership of the Commonwealth. The Commonwealth is an undefined entity of which each member is fully sovereign and independent and is committed to consulting other members without necessarily holding the same views on every problem. In the United Nations and in other spheres of international relations there have arisen occasions where Pakistan and, for that matter, other members of the Commonwealth, have taken up entirely independent attitudes, sometimes even opposed to the policies adopted by Great Britain. In doing so Pakistan has always been guided by her own interests as well as her sense of justice and fair play, and on many occasions had to vote against the views expressed by representatives of Great Britain. It is, however, felt that membership of the Commonwealth has certain advantages. One of them, perhaps, is that there are ample opportunities of co-operation in matters of common interest. This does not mean any subservience or dependence. Indeed, if Pakistan finds that membership of the Commonwealth means any loss of sovereignty or compromise of principles of public policy there would be such strong feeling against remaining in the Commonwealth that no government would be able to resist it.

The government in Pakistan is organized on a democratic basis, because democracy is deeply entrenched in the temperament of the people. The religion of the overwhelming majority is Islam, whose social structure and ideology emphasize the ideal of the equality and brotherhood of man. These feelings are fully reflected in the social and political structure of the country. Nowhere in the world, perhaps, are the highest officials and ministers of the State so unassuming and democratic in their social instincts and contacts. The people are sturdy and independent, but they have a sense of discipline. These are good auguries for democracy. The social structure, excepting for the Hindus, is completely free from the inhibitions and inequalities of the caste system. All men are considered to be equal; before law and in administration, they are treated as such. The only differences are based upon economic factors and here, too, the barriers are not as stringent or exclusive as elsewhere. The majority of the nation consists of sturdy peasants. The big landlords and industrialists form a small minority. In a society like this it would be difficult to create artificial barriers. Wealth and position have their reward in comfort and power, but they do not create social barriers between man and man. Thus a democratic form of government is in accordance with the aspirations and temperament of the people.

Pakistan faced considerable constitutional and legal difficulties as the result of Governor-General Ghulam Muhammad's action in dissolving the First Constituent Assembly; for some time it appeared that both democracy and the rule of law might receive serious setbacks; but the common sense of the people overcame the difficulties. With a view to avoiding ruinous conflict, the matter was taken to the highest court in the country which saved the situation. Thus what had threatened to jeopardize democracy, in the end resulted in the election of a new Constituent Assembly, which was more representative of current opinion, and the enactment of the Constitution. The disciplined manner in which an ugly situation was handled in spite of grave provocation and resentment reflected credit upon the people. Similarly the differences between Western Pakistan and Eastern Pakistan have been dealt with in a realistic and democratic manner; neither side has tried to impose its will on the other. At every stage there has been a compromise; in a way it was good that the teething troubles of democracy came before the constitution was enacted, otherwise the framers of the constitution, in their first enthusiasm, might have tended to ignore the realities, which would have created more serious difficulties later. A federal constitution is always a compromise between national and local loyalties; nine years had shown where the stresses might arise and it was now possible to take them into consideration. It is generally the first few years of a federation which are the most difficult and the experience of those early years was a definite asset in framing the constitution.

There is one factor in the polity of Pakistan which should be mentioned. The Pakistanis are conscious of the fact that they are a Muslim people. This feeling does not express itself in any narrow-mindedness or intolerance. It certainly does not entail any persecution of the non-Muslims. The Pakistanis, however, are desirous that they should build up a polity which breathes the very spirit of Islam. Their religion, to the Muslims in Pakistan, implies tolerance, brotherhood of man, justice, fair play and the highest moral values of life. They are strong believers in social justice. These values they want to translate into practice by establishing a polity which should be an embodiment of the

principles which they hold dear. It is because of an innate desire
to create a system of government where human dignity is fully
recognized that the Muslims demand the incorporation of Islamic
principles into their constitution. As has already been mentioned,
this by no means implies the creation of a theocracy.

Politics plays a most important part in the life of the nation.
Its one concern during the last few decades was to achieve independence. It has continuously struggled to be free alike from
the dominance of the British and the Hindus, and in this struggle
every individual had to participate. For the establishment of
Pakistan millions of her people had to make the most stupendous
sacrifices. A million people were killed for the simple reason that
they had demanded a separate statehood. More than seven
million refugees left their homes and hearths and migrated into
Pakistan in a condition, very often, of destitution. There is hardly
a family amongst the refugees which has not lost a son, a daughter,
an aged father or a relation in the great uprising against the
Muslims in several parts of India in 1947. There are some people
who are the sole survivors of large families. Many a refugee,
having trod a weary path, reached the border of Pakistan only
to fall dead with joy at having reached the promised land. A
nation which has suffered like this cannot but be politically conscious. In the humblest home people discuss politics and even
world affairs as they are likely to affect the welfare of their new-
born state. Political consciousness does not, however, necessarily
mean political maturity, which will come only with experience.
This is a potential source of weakness in an otherwise stable
polity.

CHAPTER V

Economic Institutions and Aspirations

THE Indo-Pakistan sub-continent with its 700,000 villages has always been and remains to this day predominantly agricultural. Before the full impact of foreign rule began to be felt, its economy could most appropriately be described as a village economy. The rise of modern industry with large concentration of population in urban areas is only a recent growth. In the Hindu period communications were undeveloped and, therefore, large-scale trading was difficult. The export trade was, therefore, naturally limited and the volume of internal trade much too small to have great economic significance. Each village was an economic unit in itself, self-sufficient in its meagre needs. The Muslims understood the importance of good communications and they built a number of trunk roads connecting the different provinces of their extensive empire. They organized and maintained an excellent postal system and gave great impetus to internal trade. Under their fostering care India built up, in addition, a flourishing export trade. The Indian ports were full of mediaeval ships built in India and connecting her with China in the East and Europe in the West through Egypt. In the 16th century came European traders who captured this trade from the hands of the Arabs and the Chinese, but indirectly they were instrumental in giving further impetus to the export trade of the sub-continent. As the result of this activity industry made spectacular progress. But this was not the age of the machine and, therefore, all the goods which India exported were manufactured by human labour. Her main exports were cloth, leather goods, sugar and sugar products.

Industry brought such profits that, in spite of the meagre population, the Muslim Government had to utilize all methods short of sheer coercion to keep up the agricultural produce. The expansion of agriculture to feed the growing population and to supply raw materials to the industry was one of the main anxieties of Muslim rulers in India, because a large proportion of the population had taken to industry. This is easily intelligible if it is taken into consideration that India was responsible for clothing practically all the peoples living on the littoral of the Indian Ocean and the south-western coast of the Pacific. India also supplied these areas with leather goods, sugar and indigo dyes. Besides, practically the entire West Asia depended upon India for the manufacture of seagoing vessels. All this industrial activity brought great prosperity to the Indo-Muslim Empire, but it also took away large sections of population from agriculture. In those days large-scale manufacture could be achieved only by diverting a very large proportion of population to industry. Big production at that time was naturally dependent upon large-scale cottage industries, though factories where a large number of labourers were employed were not unknown. Handicrafts flourished all over India, especially in towns where they could be sure of receiving royal patronage. Hand-spinning and weaving were ubiquitous. Dacca, now the capital of East Pakistan, was renowned for the fine quality of its muslin. Silk products came only after cotton fabrics in importance. Kashmir and the Punjab were famous centres of woollen industry. Metalwork, enamelled jewellery, stone and wood-carving were other handicrafts of considerable importance. In all these, excellence of design and artistic beauty mattered more than mere quantity.

The establishment of political authority throughout the length and breadth of this vast territory was the first and immediate concern of the British. Without easy and adequate means of communication, political control was impossible. Their energies were, therefore, directed towards building up a network of roads and railways so that their armies could be moved to centres of revolt and rebellion with great speed. But politics is always a handmaid of economics. The exploitation of economic resources in the country was the aim of British imperialism as it has been of many other imperialisms. Access to the interior meant that raw materials could be carried to the ports and from there shipped to foreign destinations. It also meant that their manfactured goods could be taken to distant parts of the sub-continent. The British came to India as traders and became rulers, and as rulers they governed the country in the interest of their trade. Sometimes this resulted in harsh measures. The handloom industry of Dacca was, for instance, the victim of British rapacity and died an unnatural death before fair competition could destroy it.

The main source of demand for handicraft products in the urban areas dried up with the disappearance of princely courts. The new bourgeoisie which replaced the old nobility was moulding its life on the Western pattern. The dominant ideas of a society are the ideas of its ruling class. With the spread of English education, Western ideas were rapidly infiltrating into the country. The habits of thought and modes of life were fast becoming Westernized. Everything foreign became fashionable and all that was native and indigenous was regarded as inferior. The new order, which had supplanted the old, created an unprecedented demand for foreign cloth and luxuries. The result was that many trades and industries succumbed before the onrush of this new tide. Some of them decayed and died; others continued to languish for want of proper finance and organization; some have survived to this day. The Dacca muslin industry had already died; ornamental work done on weapons of war in the lands that now constitute Western Pakistan perished with the prohibition of carrying arms. The shawl and woollen industries did not entirely escape the fate of others. Thus the place of pride which handicrafts had occupied in the economy of the sub-continent had gone for ever; they were never to be restored to their pristine importance.

The beginning of modern industry in India dates from the middle of the 19th century. Cotton and jute mills were among the first to be established. By gradual stages, through periods of prosperity and depression, these two industries developed to such an extent that they came to occupy a prominent position in the economy of India in the present century. The iron and steel industry too began to take root immediately before the outbreak of the First World War. This war, which cut off foreign supplies, especially from the West, gave a great fillip to Indian industry. A host of light and medium industries developed. Without heavy industry this development was, however, bound to be lopsided. Machinery had to come from abroad. In another sense too this development was unsound. Most of the industry, especially that of cotton and jute, developed near the ports. Bombay became the hub of cotton industry and Calcutta of jute. The development of these industries in and around the port areas, away from the centres of the production of raw materials as also from large markets for consumption, was partly due to the anarchy of private enterprise. There was no planning or planned development. The result was that when the sub-continent was partitioned, Pakistan, which produced 30 per cent. of the total output of raw cotton— 75 per cent. of which is of superior American variety—and 75 per cent. of jute in pre-partition India, had hardly any factories for manufacturing these raw materials into finished goods. Jute mills were non-existent and out of nearly 430 cotton mills only fourteen fell to the share of Pakistan, twelve of which were located in East Bengal, which produces very little cotton, and two in Western Pakistan, which is the fourth largest exporter of raw cotton in the world. In fact, before the Partition the raw cotton of Western Pakistan and the raw jute of East Bengal were travelling to Bombay and Calcutta. Part of the cotton cloth manufactured in Bombay was sent back to the areas now constituting Pakistan, and the jute which earned most of India's foreign exchange was sent through Calcutta. The fact that predominantly Muslim areas were consigned to the production of raw materials for Hindu industry was one of the major factors in the struggle for Pakistan.

Agriculture, therefore, remains the most important industry of Pakistan. It is the base upon which the entire economic structure rests. It provides the means of living, in one way or another, for nearly 90 per cent. of the population. It provides the foreign exchange for buying consumer and capital goods for the satisfaction of immediate demands and future needs of the population. The total area under food and commercial crops is 49 million acres, only 10 per cent. of which is under non-food crops.[1]

The character of agriculture and the nature of the crops grown in the two regions of Pakistan are very different. The majority of

FOOD CROPS IN 1954-55

[1] COMMODITIES	ACRES	PRODUCTION (tons)
Rice	23,700,000	8,405,000
Wheat	10,661,000	3,172,000
Gram	3,102,000	632,000
Bajra	2,200,000	346,000
Rape and Mustard	1,803,000	324,000
Jawar	1,119,000	217,000
Maize	1,068,000	440,000
Sugarcane ...	1,017,000	1,228,000 (raw sugar)
Barley	568,000	141,000

continued on p. 51

the area in Western Pakistan is watered by an excellent system of irrigation canals, while in Eastern Pakistan agriculture is mostly dependent on the monsoons. Western Pakistan specializes in wheat and cotton; jute and rice are the products of Eastern Pakistan.

Despite the overwhelming importance of agriculture in the economy of the sub-continent, the standard of living of the vast majority of the rural population was very low—almost below the margin of subsistence. Apart from lack of mechanization and absence of chemical manuring, two factors in the social system had largely contributed to their poverty. The growing pressure of population on land combined with the laws of inheritance had progressively reduced the size of agricultural holdings. The greater number of holdings cultivated by peasant proprietors were too small to make agriculture a paying proposition.

There were a little more than 900,000 owners in the Punjab who owned lands below five acres each and 1,130,000 owners owned lands which were below ten acres per holding.[1] In the North-West Frontier Province, where 42 per cent. of the culti- vated land (1,048,523 acres) belonged to peasant proprietors, conditions were very similar. Both in the Punjab and the North- West Frontier Province the size of holdings was uneconomic. There were few peasant proprietors in Sind, which is even to-day full of landlords. Pakistan is making Herculean efforts to remove

[1] The size of the holdings in the Punjab is well illustrated by the following table:

GROUP	NO. OF OWNERS (Figures in millions)	ACREAGE
Up to 5 acres	·906	1·80
5 to 10 acres	·227	1·60
10 to 15 acres	·052	·80
15 to 25 acres	·064	1·35
25 to 100 acres	·065	1·45
Above 100 acres	·036	·80
Total	1·350	7·80

NON-FOOD CROPS		
COMMODITIES	ACRES	PRODUCTION (tons)
Jute	1,150,000	484,000
Cotton	3,185,000	279,000
Tea	74,000	24,000
Sesamum	212,000	36,000
Linseed	76,000	14,000
Tobacco	235,000	115,000

these evils by expanding her irrigation and settling colonies of peasants in newly-developed areas.

The besetting evil which Pakistan's agriculture has inherited is the dominating place which the landlord occupies in rural economy. There was no landlordism in the days of Muslim rule; there was direct relationship between the cultivator and the state. The divorce between the ownership of the land and the cultivator is a product of the British rule and a recent growth in the history of this sub-continent. The first foundations of landlordism were laid in 1793 by Lord Cornwallis, who imposed the Permanent Settlement creating a class of hereditary landlords under which the peasantry of Bengal has continued to groan to this day. " The traditions of Bengal were transplanted to the rest of India as the virus of British infection travelled deeper into our body-politic." [1] The magnitude of the evil can best be visualized from the fact that in the Punjab more than 50 per cent., in the North-West Frontier Province a little less than 50 per cent. and in Sind over 90 per cent. agricultural land is owned by non-cultivating, rent-receiving landlords. The tenants who work on these lands have little security of tenure and no statutory rights, liable to be evicted by the landlords at their own sweet will. Then there are the *jagirdars* who acquired land from the British in return for the services they had rendered to the cause of imperialism. Their estates are free from all encumbrances and they pay no revenue to the State.

The reform of the land system in Pakistan has, therefore, assumed primary importance. Various official and non-official bodies have investigated into the working of the system and recommended measures of reform.

Though there are differences of opinion on the extent and the speed with which the change should be brought about, all are unanimous in their view that the system is in need of immediate reform. *Jagirdari* has already been abolished in the North-West Frontier Province without compensation; and occupancy tenants (who cultivated 11 per cent. of the area in that province) have been given the right to acquire the full ownership of their holdings. The Punjab has recently reformed its

[1] *Report of the Agrarian Committee appointed by the Working Committee of the Pakistan Muslim League* (p. 12).

20. A Hill Man Ploughing his Fields

21. A Harvest Scene

22. JUTE BEING TAKEN FOR BALING

23. COTTON BEING BROUGHT TO A MILL

tenancy laws, the results of which can be assessed only after some time. The Floud Commission appointed in 1940 to inquire into the effects of the Permanent Settlement had recommended complete abolition of landlordism in Bengal. On the basis of their recommendations, the East Pakistan Government has, after obtaining legal authority, started taking over the estates. The Agrarian Committee appointed by the Muslim League for West Pakistan has proposed a gradual elimination of landlordism and the establishment of peasant proprietorship. They have recommended a minimum holding of twenty-five acres and cultivation of land on a co-operative basis on modern scientific lines.

Vigorous efforts are being made by the Government to increase the area under cultivation through large-scale irrigation projects, reclamation and prevention of soil erosion all over the country. The Lower Sind Barrage has been completed; the Thal Project in the Punjab has made great progress and colonies planted in this area which was a desert are now thriving. Other projects are in various stages of development in Baluchistan, East Bengal, the North-West Frontier and Bahawalpur. Over six million acres of barren and waste lands will be added to the existing cultivable area in the next few years, thus augmenting the food and raw material resources of Pakistan.

Even this will not relieve the growing pressure of population. There is too much concealed unemployment and under employment on land. New avenues of employment have to be found or created to absorb the surplus population. In this background the industrial development of the country becomes an issue of immediate importance for the economic future of Pakistan.

Though Pakistan has a great industrial potential, the industrial capacity at the time of Partition was insignificant. Among thirty-four factories there were fourteen cotton and nine sugar mills, five glass and five cement factories.

There is a bright future for cotton, wool, jute and leather industries. The raw materials are available in abundance. The output of cotton is 1,300,000 bales of the long staple American variety. Pakistan produces jute of superior quality and the annual production amounts to seven million bales. Pakistan produces twenty-two million pounds of good wool, to which another eleven million should be added which is brought by the nomads who come from across the border. The annual production of hides and skins is ten million pieces. At the time of the Partition the entire jute crop, most of the raw cotton, hides and skins and wool were exported abroad. The absence of industry made Pakistan unduly dependent on foreign sources even for finished goods manufactured from these raw materials.

The Government, therefore, adopted a policy for developing those industries for which abundant raw material was available in the country. For the purposes of proper planning a certain degree of control for procuring capital goods has been considered necessary. But apart from the issue of foreign exchange for the purchase of capital goods from abroad, no restrictions have been imposed upon the establishment of industry or its ownership or management. A small number of industries like the generation of hydro-electric power, the manufacture of railway locomotives and wagons, of the apparatus needed for telephones, telegraphic and wireless communications, and of military equipment, and broadcasting are to be owned and managed by the State. The establishment of a statutory body, called the Pakistan Industrial Development Corporation, which functions as a commercial concern, has given great impetus to industry. This Corporation promotes industrial undertakings of a basic nature in co-operation with private capital, and when an industry is well established it gradually withdraws by selling the stocks in the open market. The remaining field of the economy is to be left for development by private enterprise. The State will, of course, take measures to stop the exploitation of the worker and prevent low wages or unhealthy living conditions. All possible assistance to private enterprise is promised. Some help has already been given by lowering the import duty on machinery from 10 to 5 per cent. A special depreciation charge has been allowed on new ventures, and profits below 5 per cent. of the capital are exempt from income tax for a period of five years. An industrial Finance Corporation (to which Government has subscribed 51 per cent. of the capital) has been set up to advance long-term credit to industry. Industrial estates have been established in Karachi and Hyderabad and similar estates have been planned for other towns. These estates will provide assistance in the location of factories, warehouses, electric power, water and railway sidings. They will also help the Government in implementing its policy of dispersing industry and preventing its concentration in a few over-crowded centres.

Foreign capital which enters Pakistan for purely economic and industrial objectives is welcome. It will enjoy all the advantages available to indigenous capital and the restrictions on remittance of profits will only be of a general nature incidental to exchange limitations. There are some industries in which indigenous capital should have a 51 per cent. share; there are others in which its minimum share has been prescribed as 30 per cent. But these restrictions can be relaxed if indigenous capital is unable to subscribe its quota.

At the time of Partition, Pakistan had fourteen cotton textile mills, 166,000 spindles and 4,450 looms. Their production capacity was $76\frac{1}{2}$ million yards. Together with the output of handlooms the production of cloth amounted to 90 million yards. It was wholly inadequate to satisfy the home demand of nearly 1,150 million yards annually. Cotton textile industry has now made such rapid strides that Pakistan is very near achieving self-sufficiency. It is already producing all the coarse and medium quality cloth consumed in the country; it has also built up an export trade in these qualities as well as in yarn. Only small quantities of superfine quality are imported. Pakistan started with one woollen mill of 2,000 spindles. Now Pakistan is able to manufacture all the woollen cloth that the country needs. Pakistan possessed no jute mills, not even sufficient facilities for baling. To-day baling facilities are adequate and several jute mills have gone into production. One of these is the largest unit in the world. The products of these mills are of excellent quality and compete successfully with the products of other countries. The shoe industry in Pakistan has made spectacular progress. To-day Pakistan imports no shoes and has an exportable surplus. Pakistan has also achieved self-sufficiency in the manufacture of matches and is able to export cement. The production of sugar has greatly increased and apart from other smaller units there is a giant plant, the biggest in Asia, at Mardan which has an annual production of 50,000 tons. Similarly a large paper mill has been established in East Pakistan to utilize the great reserves of bamboo pulp in Chittagong hill tracts and Sylhet. This mill along with another plant in Khulna will make

Pakistan self-sufficient in paper. A strawboard factory newly constructed at Nowshehra now meets all Pakistan's requirements in that commodity. The tobacco industry has made rapid strides and Pakistan is to-day self-sufficient in cigarettes. A number of smaller industries have also grown. The sports goods industry at Sialkot in Punjab has a well-established reputation for quality and craftsmanship. Its goods find a good market in Britain, Australia, New Zealand, America Switzerland and Belgium. Sialkot also possesses a thriving industry for the manufacture of surgical instruments which find a ready market in many countries of the world. Pakistan hitherto lacked heavy industry because the deposits of iron had not been discovered. Recently deposits of excellent quality have been discovered in West Pakistan and plans to build up an iron and steel industry are well in hand. The deposits of coal are being worked but most of the coal is of an inferior quality. However, recently a large underground reservoir of natural gas has been discovered and pipe-lines have now been laid to bring it to Karachi and various other important centres in Sind and Punjab. Moreover, a giant thermal plant for producing energy is being set up in Baluchistan which will consume this gas and provide electricity for large areas of the Punjab and Baluchistan. It will also make it possible to work the iron deposits. It is expected that industrial development will gain a great impetus by the availability of this cheap fuel. The production of petroleum, chromite, gypsum and fertilizers has been speeded up. Large schemes for producing hydro-electric power have been executed in the North-West Frontier and the Punjab. The power houses at Malakand, Dargai and Rasul produce more than 50,000 kilowatts. The multipurpose schemes at Warsak and Karnaphuli already under execution will produce 100,000 and 60,000 kilowatts respectively. There are a number of other smaller projects.

This record of industrial progress within the space of a few years, if not spectacular, is by no means insignificant. It should justify hopes of a rapid advance in the future. Pakistan's balanced budgets and its production of commodities needed in the hard-currency areas, are great assets to the nation. Stable political conditions and the expanding phase of the economy should prove good inducement for foreign capital to seek entry into Pakistan for developing her latent wealth.

Handicrafts are still the source of employment to a small proportion of the population. Pakistani craftsmen are known for their artistic sense and exquisite workmanship. The Government is taking interest in them and training centres have been established at various places for increasing production. A Finance Corporation to give impetus to cottage industries is being established. Some co-operative societies also have been formed for the purpose of putting these handicrafts on a sound economic basis. Pottery, enamel work, jewellery, silver work and brassware produced by Pakistani artisans achieve a high standard of craftsmanship. There is also a thriving handloom industry. Apart from cotton cloth, carpets of good workmanship also are produced. The total number of persons employed solely as craftsmen is not very large. Some of the work is done in their spare time by peasant families.

Before the Partition, commerce was almost entirely in the hands of Hindu merchants who, from West Pakistan, migrated to India. The Muslims, therefore, had to step into their shoes and within a short period they proved themselves equal to the task. They prevented the economy of Pakistan from falling into chaos and thus rendered a great service to the nation. To-day no one who visits Pakistan for the first time can even imagine that the present shops and trading houses did not originally belong to their present owners or that a very large percentage of them are entirely new. This shows the remarkable adaptability of the Pakistani people to new circumstances and is a happy augury for its progress.

The State is still the largest employer not only because it is responsible for the administration of a big country but also because the railways are nationalized. As has already been mentioned, all the civil and military services are manned by Pakistanis themselves except just a few posts which are held by Britishers who did not choose to retire after independence. They are mostly to be found in the army. Such posts, as soon as they fall vacant, are filled by Pakistani nationals.

The distribution of national income is naturally unequal. The big merchants, landlords and some of the ruling princes are wealthy. The mass of the people is poor. This is due, as has already been explained, to the presence of landlords and the small size of the holdings of the cultivators. The standard of living, so far as the wealthier classes are concerned, compares favourably with the standard in other countries; the poor have few amenities of life. When crops are good the people have plenty to eat and there is no shortage of cloth either. But other comforts are unknown to an average villager.

The industrial régime in Pakistan is based upon the principle of free enterprise. As has been mentioned, only a few industries have been nationalized. In an industrially backward area planning is absolutely essential. But planning does not rule out freedom of enterprise. The workers are organized in trade unions. The craftsmen who work independently have their own guilds. The trade unions are effective organizations and they do not hesitate in enforcing their demands with the usual methods of protests and strikes if their interests are adversely affected. The Government has been so liberal that some classes of government servants have also organized their trade unions. Amongst these the most effective unions are those of postal workers and the workers on the railways. Even the clerks, office boys and others have their organizations, because the Government does not discourage trade unions. There is considerable liberal legislation on the Statute Book to guarantee the rights of workers, including the right of organization. The peasants also have their organizations for agitating for the recognition of their rights. Their strength is a reflex of the presence of big landlords and the absence of adequate rights of tenancy. Sind, which is the worst affected part of the country, has also the most flourishing peasant organization. The *Hari Haqdar* organization, which translated into English means "the Association for the Enforcement of Peasants' Rights," has a large membership and there is hardly a village of any importance where it has not established a local committee and an office. This organization publishes a newspaper called *Hari Haqdar*.

The Pakistanis, on the whole, are staunch believers in the principles of social justice and their tendencies would be described in many countries as leftist. This does not mean that they are Communists, because most of the people are ardent Muslims and do not believe in the Marxist theory of materialism. Their sense of social justice is born of their faith in Islam. Thus they inherently believe in the fundamental equality and rights

of the individual. The democratic social order of Islam in itself
is a potent factor in producing this feeling. There has been some
manoeuvring on the part of landlords to neutralize the Government's zeal for reforms. But few among them have the courage to
come out in the open and defend landlordism blatantly. The
landlords realize that a progressive country cannot long maintain
them in power or in a privileged position. The workers and the
peasants understand the progressive trends in the country and are
fully confident of their ultimate success. In the absence of large-
scale industry, labour unrest is not a common feature of life, but
within the spheres where large-scale labour plays a part there
is continuous pressure for better wages and conditions of service.
As the State has shown liberal leanings, it has won the affection
of the peasants and the workers. The employers are not unaware
of this liberal trend and they do not resent it. The only group
which shows resistance is that of the big landlords, and their
opposition in West Pakistan has put a brake on the progress of
the peasants towards emancipation. The need for agrarian reform,
however, has been emphasized in the First Five Years Plan; it is
gradually emerging as the most important issue in political think-
ing. East Pakistan has already abolished landlordism; but even
there it will take the provincial government some time to disen-
tangle all the complexities of an intricate system of subinfeudation
created in the course of two centuries.

Recently the Communists have shown considerable activity.
The Communist Party of Pakistan has a small membership;
nevertheless it is active. They mostly work amongst the students
and try to capture labour unions. They do not avowedly preach
the doctrines of Communism except to a chosen few; they, however, endeavour to exploit minor grievances and create a general
sense of frustration. They even pose as better Muslims than those
in authority because they preach extreme interpretation of the
doctrines of Islamic brotherhood and social justice and thus pre-
pare the ground for the acceptance of Marxist doctrines. They
have a well-defined programme of infiltration into important
institutions for the purpose of creating cells of workers for leaven-
ing public opinion with Communist beliefs. The people of
Pakistan will not accept Communism so long as the policies of
the State remain liberal and loyalty to Islam continues. But in

a country where literacy is low and the sense of liberty and equality is inherent in the psychology of the people who still lack political experience and maturity, Communism is a grave potential danger. With the intensification of the efforts of the Communists there has been growing a wariness against its subtle methods which is steadily developing into hostility.

CHAPTER VI

Religious Institutions and Aspirations

IN Western Pakistan the earliest record of religious beliefs is to be found in the excavations of Mohenjo Daro and Harappa. It is revealed at Mohenjo Daro that some kind of *Shaivite* worship was perhaps in vogue. This is only a conjecture, because some images, mostly in terra-cotta, have been discovered which bear extraordinary resemblance to the head of Shiva as executed by the later schools of the *Shaivite* religion. With the inroads of the Aryans it seems that the religious beliefs underwent a change, but the older traditions do not seem to have been completely wiped out. The Aryans occupied a major part of the northern portion of Western Pakistan, where a good many hymns of the Vedas seem to have been composed. The Vedic religion put greater emphasis on right action as distinguished from right belief and emotional fervour; it consisted mostly of elaborate forms of ritual. It was believed that so long as these forms were maintained and followed the prosperity of the individual and the community was assured and happiness in the next life was guaranteed. With the growth of time, and as the result of contacts with the indigenous population which had achieved a higher standard of civilization, the Aryans developed tendencies of philosophic speculation as well as an emotional devotion to a deity or an idealized mythological or historical character. The tendency to lay the greater emphasis on action, however, persisted.

Ultimately there came to be recognized three ways of attaining salvation which, in accordance with the Indo-Aryan philosophy, was freedom from the cycle of birth and re-birth. The fundamental of this philosophy was that the chain of cause and effect in the form of action and its punishment or reward did not come to an end in the first life and, therefore, the soul had to be born again and again in the world to atone for its misdeeds. Life in this world implied pain and suffering and the real release from pain would come only through freedom from birth and re-birth. This fundamental notion runs throughout Hindu philosophy, and all schools of religion which had their birth in this sub-continent seem to have taken it for granted. Salvation, that is to say, freedom from birth and re-birth, therefore, was a consequence of right action, because it was right action alone which could produce the correct effect of ultimate deliverance from suffering. Gradually, and as the result of the contribution of the more ancient indigenous thought, Brahminism developed three schools of thought. The first and the most ancient, which believed in the potency of right action in the attainment of salvation, came to be called *Karma Marga* or the path of action. The speculative philosophers, however, said that the basis for all correct action could be only knowledge, and therefore knowledge was superior to action. It was necessary, according to this school, for the human mind to obtain the fullest knowledge which alone could open to him the door of salvation. This school of thought was called *Gñana Marga* or the path of knowledge. The third school, which betrays to a deeper extent the contribution of ancient indigenous Indian thought, held that knowledge alone is not sufficient and that the real guiding power is devotion without which the human mind cannot attune itself to the dictates of duty. This was known as *Bhakti Marga* or the path of devotion. The Brahminical religion, however, remained mostly ritualistic and the path of action was always dominant and had the largest number of followers.

The fact that the Aryans had a lighter complexion than the indigenous population made the new conquerors colour-conscious and they took rigorous steps to maintain their race superiority. The Indo-Aryans developed a philosophy of a hereditary functional society which assigned various stations in life to persons in accordance with their birth. This was called *Varna*, which literally means colour. Thus the caste system amongst the Hindus is really the outcome of colour consciousness. The main characteristic of caste is that it divides society into groups which, perhaps, in the beginning were not so rigid, but later it became impossible for any person to outstep the limits imposed by caste.

Anyone belonging to one caste could not become a member of another. He could, of course, become an outcaste; but then he was assigned to the lowest rung of the society. The four main castes, in the order of their precedence, were : the priestly caste called the Brahmins, the rulers and warriors called Kshatriyas, the merchants and tradespeople who were called Vaishyas and the serving classes and manual labourers were called Sudras. Those who could not be fitted into these castes were outcastes and were not permitted to live inside the town. Actually every caste had its separate quarter and sometimes even Sudras had to live outside the walled township.

The rigidity of the caste system was greatly resented by some thinkers and, mainly as the reaction to the injustice of this system, there arose two other schools of thought. One of these was founded by the prince Gautama, who became Buddha after attaining enlightenment. This system is called Buddhism and commands a large number of adherents in many Asiatic countries. The other school is called Jainism, whose main teacher was Mahavira. The two systems are very much alike in their insistence upon non-violence and their desire and endeavour to escape the chain of birth, death and re-birth through *Nirvana* or self-immolation. At the time of the Muslim conquest of the areas now included in Pakistan, the religion of a large number of inhabitants was still some form of Buddhism, but Brahminism had achieved power, because it became the religion of the ruling classes. Actually Buddhism had divided itself into two schools, the Hinayana and Mahayana. Hinayana, literally the lesser path, was nearer to the teachings of Gautama, and Mahayana, literally the great path, was diluted with idolatrized Hinduism.

Among the Hindus, as the result of certain practices developed under certain speculative notions regarding the origin of the world, a school called *Vama Margi,* or the left path, also called *Tantrism,* had become popular. Hindu speculative thought had evolved long before this the idea of a trinity consisting of Brahma, the Creator, Vishnu, the Preserver, and Shiva, the Destroyer. This division of divine virtues and powers led a large number of Hindus into worshipping the creative power through phallic signs. The glorification and worship of the phallic signs naturally led to the belief that sexual intercourse in itself was an act of worship. This thought found its extreme expression in *Tantrism* where obscene practices and secret orgies of debauchery were looked upon as the means of salvation. The Tantric temples were covered with pictures and images of an obscene nature and some of them have still survived and are found in Eastern Pakistan. The main religion, apart from Islam, in Pakistan is Brahminism, generally called Hinduism, and a number of Hindus in East Pakistan still belong to the *Tantric* school, though they have now outgrown obscene practices and beliefs. The Buddhists form a substantial minority in East Bengal. Amongst other minorities are the Zoroastrians, who are of Persian origin and are followers of the Prophet Zoroaster. They believe in the dual principle of good and evil and look upon fire as the emblem of divine purity and power. Pakistan also has a number of Christians. A large number of these are Catholics who have mainly migrated from Goa from time to time and to-day are a flourishing community in Karachi. In East Pakistan and the rest of Pakistan there is a small Protestant population as well.

When the Arabs conquered Sind, and thus planted the banner of Islam on the soil of Pakistan, the vast majority of people were Buddhists, but the ruling dynasty was Brahmin. The Brahmins had utilized their authority to oppress and subjugate the Buddhists, who were in an unhappy position. When the Muslim invasion took place, they were apathetic to the fate of the ruling dynasty and either co-operated with the Muslim conquerors or, at best, held aloof from the war. The Muslims thus did not have much difficulty in adding a new province to the world of Islam and, having established themselves in Sind, they gradually increased their domains and established their rule on the major portion of the area which now constitutes Western Pakistan. They followed an enlightened policy towards the people of the soil with the result that large numbers of them were converted to Islam of their own free will, because in this way they achieved equality with the ruling class and were able to forget their subservience to their Brahmin masters and rulers who had oppressed them. This, apart from spiritual considerations, is the secret of the Muslim majority in Western Pakistan. Of course, the area constituting Pakistani Baluchistan had already been conquered and converted by the Arabs. Before the Ghaznawids conquered the

Punjab, in the 10th century of the Christian era, after having established their rule in Afghanistan, Multan was already a Muslim stronghold and Islam was not unknown in that province. The Ghaznawids yielded to the pressure of Saljuq Turks and ultimately had to rest content with their dominions in Punjab with Lahore as their capital. The Ghaznawids had traditions of culture and learning and Lahore grew as a centre of Muslim arts and sciences. It soon became famous as one of the main cities of Islam and references to it in early Islamic literature are numerous and flattering. Thus, fairly early in History, Islam was established in Western Pakistan.

About two centuries later a Muslim general serving under the newly-established Sultanate of Delhi, Muhammad bin Bakhtyar Khalji, conquered Bengal. Here again he found, curiously enough, more or less the same conditions as the Arabs had found in Sind. The ruling dynasty was Brahminical in religion and the vast majority of the people were Buddhists who had lost the pristine purity of their religion and followed a cult which was a corruption of Mahayana. For their religious faith they were maltreated by the Hindu rulers, and there is still literature which expresses the glee of these downtrodden people at the extinction of the power of their rulers and oppressors. They only half understood Islam, but they sing in no uncertain terms of Muhammad being the avenger of their sufferings. Amongst such a population enthusiasm for the new order which released them from a tyranny worse than death was overwhelming. This enthusiasm, once again, expressed itself in wholesale conversions to Islam, and Eastern Pakistan also became a Muslim majority area. It has seldom happened in the annals of mankind that history has repeated itself so faithfully.

It is unnecessary to describe Islam at any great length. The Muslims believe in the unity of God and they consider that He sent divinely guided Prophets for the deliverance of mankind from ignorance. The Qur'an mentions Christ and the Hebrew prophets as inspired teachers of religious truth and enjoins respect for them as well as for the prophets of other nations. Of all the prophets, the Muslims believe Muhammad to be the most perfect and the last. The reason for this belief is that they consider that Muhammad gave to the world the essence of religion which is the very eternal and immutable Truth. This truth is capable of progressive interpretation and application in accordance with the changing conditions of the world. Islam is a simple and rational faith. It does not make impossible demands upon the human reason in the realm of belief and it depends on reason for its appeal. The Muslim people are, therefore, not bound by any great shackles of dogma and are peculiarly sensitive to progress. Their outlook on life is practical and rational and their faith is more a guidance than a hindrance. The Muslims of Pakistan are known for their passionate love of Islam without betraying any traces of intolerance.

The largest group, of course, are the Muslims. In Western Pakistan the number of minorities is very small. In Eastern Pakistan the Hindus number 9,239,000, of whom 5,052,000 are Scheduled Castes. The Scheduled Castes are the people who are considered by the Hindus to be outside the pale of castes and the very touch and sometimes even the shadow of one of these unfortunate human beings pollutes a Brahmin. As Islam does not believe in such distinctions, the Scheduled Castes naturally feel much happier in a Muslim country than they would in Hindu territory, in spite of the fact that they still call themselves Hindus. The importance attached by Pakistan to the Scheduled Castes is symbolized by the fact that one of them served as a member of the cabinet of the Central Government. Pakistan has granted special scholarships and facilities for the education of these backward citizens who became her charge as the result of independence. The Pakistani Scheduled Castes also are found mostly in Eastern Pakistan. In Western Pakistan their number is comparatively small.

The ruling classes, the industrialists, the merchants, the workers, the peasants are all predominantly Muslim in Western Pakistan. In Eastern Pakistan the Hindus are mostly industrialists, merchants and property-owning classes. The Scheduled Castes are backward and poor. Here the Muslims are mainly peasants and only a small proportion of them belong to the wealthier classes. The Zoroastrians, who are mostly limited to Western Pakistan, are a prosperous class and are mostly business magnates or traders. Some of them work in commercial concerns in various capacities. The Christians can be roughly divided into two classes. Those who have been converted mostly from higher castes of the Hindus or who have received modern education belong to the middle classes and are found in various professions and services. Those who have been converted from amongst the Scheduled Castes or those who have not received proper education are agriculturists or belong to humbler walks of life. There is a small number of Pakistani Jews as well, who are mostly traders.

The psychological set-up of the followers of different religions can be roughly divided into two categories, eastern and western. The Muslims, the Christians and the Jews can be said to possess the western outlook on life, rational, practical and progressive. Those who belong to the ancient religions of India have the eastern trend of mind which is speculative and conservative. In spite of differences in belief, the Buddhists and the Hindus, whether belonging to the Scheduled Castes or otherwise, tenaciously follow the ideals of ancient India. Their tendency is to be exclusive. The Hindus have a great talent for music and dancing and, when educated, their minds are subtle and speculative. They are also shrewd and highly intelligent and show considerable adaptability when confronted with new problems. The Muslims are democratic in outlook and do not tolerate the rigours of social barriers. Whatsoever be their status in life, they consider themselves to be the equals of the highest in the land. It is perhaps the result of this feeling that even the highest ministers of state in Pakistan are unassuming and sociable. When a minister or a high official goes to a mosque he is neither received nor given a special seat; he may find a seat next to a beggar or his own servant. No one will move from his place to honour him. This attitude reveals the true mental make-up of a Muslim though it does not breed in him indiscipline or lack of respect for national leaders. No people could be more passionately fond of its leader than the Muslims were of the Qaid-i-Azam, the founder of their nation. No Prime Minister could be more popular than was Mr. Liaquat Ali Khan, who was the first Prime Minister of Pakistan, and yet Muslims looked upon him only as a fellow-Muslim who had been chosen by the nation to guide its destinies.

Religion plays a most important role in the life of the Pakistani nation. The Muslims are devoted followers of Islam, the Hindus hold steadfastly to their philosophy and are devoted to their religion. The Catholics and other Christians are as pious as any Christians in the world. The general atmosphere is religious; the Pakistanis are a deeply religious people to whichever religion they might belong. It is, therefore, felt universally that politics should not be divorced completely from religion. It is widely recognized that a state based upon the eternal principles of true religion is the greatest guarantee of tolerance, justice and peace. Being themselves religious the minorities of Pakistan value the declarations of the leaders that the government should be guided by ethics of Islam. The Muslims believe that politics divorced from ethical principles is a positive danger to humanity and this feeling is shared with them by their fellow-citizens belonging to other religions. Islam guarantees the fullest protection to the religion and the customs of all minorities and ensures for them a privileged position in the State. A leader of the Christian minority once said that the best safeguard for his community was the adherence of the Muslim majority to the principles of Islam.

CHAPTER VII

The Pakistani People and the World

PAKISTAN is a new State and ever since its birth has been confronted with problems of great magnitude. As the result of widespread disorders, massacres and looting more than seven million Muslims migrated into the country from the neighbouring territories of India. It was by no means easy to rehabilitate these vast numbers and a good deal of the energy of the Government and the people had to be diverted towards this problem. The rehabilitation of refugees has made rapid strides; to-day there are no refugees left in camps waiting to be resettled. This does not, however, mean that the problem of rehabilitation has been solved, because after the fulfilment of the immediate physical needs there are a large number of psychological problems which require careful adjustment. It cannot be claimed that all refugees have found employment, but there are very few, comparatively speaking, who have no means of sustenance or who do not possess a shelter. When it is taken into consideration that these refugees were rehabilitated without the help of any international agency, it would be understood what constructive spirit Pakistani nationalism possesses. The only help that Pakistan received was that some foreign medical missions worked at the time of great stress, but this contribution, though valuable, was like a drop in the ocean. Unfortunately the migration of Muslims from India has not stopped and a trickle continues which keeps the problem alive and causes grave anxiety to the Government and the people.

Another test of the constructive genius of the Pakistani people was the establishment of proper government. Pakistan started from scratch. With the Partition the various services were disorganized and the Central Government did not possess even a proper secretariat. It is literally true that there were no chairs, no tables, no stationery, practically nothing. To this may be added the inconvenience of the absence of statistics or reliable figures of any kind. There was complete chaos. This chaos prevailed practically everywhere in local and provincial governments as well as the central government. Within a short period, however, the machinery was put into gear and the various organs of the State began to function smoothly as if there had been no dislocation. This in itself is an achievement which deserves commendation.

The economic life of the country was equally disorganized. There were many railway stations without staff and many skilled workers without work. The shops were empty, the factories were deserted because a large number of Hindus in Western Pakistan had chosen to migrate. The people, however, stepped into the shoes of those who had left and to-day the economic life of the country is not only normal, but has even registered considerable progress. The pace of development in the fields of industry and agricultural projects has been remarkable. Pakistan is an orderly, disciplined and well-organized country with a progressive economy and a stable currency. Its economy has been occasionally subjected to strains arising from large-scale droughts and devastating floods; in spite of such setbacks, it has, on the whole, shown considerable vitality. This reflects great credit, as has been said, on the constructive genius of the people.

Another grave problem before the people is the question of Kashmir which hitherto has baffled solution. The people of Kashmir want accession to Pakistan and the Pakistani people consider the people of Kashmir as their own kith and kin. Pakistan desires nothing better than a fair plebiscite so that the people of Kashmir may be able to express their choice unhampered by the military domination of a foreign power. Sentiment regarding Kashmir is very strong and yet the people of Pakistan want a peaceful, just and fair solution. This would show that the people of Pakistan are peace-abiding and want to co-operate with the world in building up peace.

The majority of the Pakistanis are Muslims and Islam believes in the dignity of the individual and his freedom. There is no regimentation in Islam; therefore, the people of Pakistan are remarkably free from totalitarian tendencies. The democratic social system of Islam has bred in Pakistan a people fully conscious of its freedom and tolerant to individual opinions and actions. One has to live among the people to understand how important the role of the individual is, who does not like any shackles on his freedom unless he himself considers them necessary for the purpose of the maintenance of public order and the fabric of the State. There is no idealization of the State, the Government or the national leaders. The Press and the people criticize the government openly if they disagree with its policy in any matter. A people which is so independent, sturdy and free from emotional complexes could hardly do otherwise. Individual liberty, therefore, plays an important role in the life of the country; there is no subservience of the individual to any group, whether the family or the nation.

There is considerable regional patriotism. This is inevitable in a country where different languages are spoken and each language has its own literature of which the people are proud. As the result of different languages there are variations in local culture, which are a source of pride to the groups concerned; even the variations in the cookery from one region to another evoke affection. But regional patriotism does not override the dictates of nationalism; in spite of the fact that Eastern Pakistan is so far away from Western Pakistan and in Western Pakistan itself there are so many different groups, the national feeling is genuine and strong. The people are fully conscious of national unity and the need for maintaining it, because of the dangers to which they are exposed on account of their geographical situation. The name of Pakistan embodies this sense of national unity and is a word to conjure with; so that even the tribes on the north-west frontier which had a record of internecine jealousy and warfare have united in their desire to serve Pakistan. The greatest miracle of the establishment of Pakistan is the achievement of peace on the north-west frontier and the willingness of different tribes to sink their differences for a higher cause.

Foreigners have always felt at home in this country and the reason is the innate courtesy of the people of Pakistan and their friendliness towards people of all nations and countries. A foreigner is looked upon as an honoured guest and practically everyone goes out of his way to help him and to befriend him. The people of Pakistan do not forget their courtesy even in the face of grave provocation. So far as the neighbours of Pakistan are concerned, relations with India tend to be strained and, at present, unhappy. In spite of the happenings before and after the Partition, which have greatly embittered the relations between the two countries, Indian citizens travelling through Pakistan receive utmost courtesy and consideration. So far as the inhabitants of Muslim countries are concerned, they are shown all affection, because Pakistan feels the strength of the bonds of a common religion with these countries. The people of Burma and Ceylon are looked upon as allies and friends. American and European visitors are treated hospitably and with friendliness. Actually it would be difficult to find a more friendly and courteous people. Those foreigners who have lived for any length of time in any part of Pakistan have been greatly impressed by the lack of prejudice against foreigners.

This refers, of course, to people of different countries as individuals. So far as ethnical or linguistic communities are concerned, the opinion of the Pakistani is based upon his political or social relations with them. A community or a country in the abstract is to an average Pakistani quite different from the sum total of its individuals. It is possible, for instance, that the policy of a country may be disliked by the people of Pakistan and yet its individuals treated with the same courtesy as the individuals of other nations. Amongst the neighbours of Pakistan, as has already been said, relations with India are not happy and Indian policy in Kashmir and towards the Muslim minority left in India is considered to be unjust and harsh. The Muslims in Pakistan feel very strongly on these points and, therefore, it is not to be expected that they would look upon India with affection. Ceylon and Burma are looked upon as allies, being potentially in the same position as Pakistan is in relation to the great neighbour India, which is suspected of nursing a growing imperialism against her neighbours. The attitude of Afghanistan also was, for several years, unfriendly, but it was universally recognized that both the government and people of Pakistan showed unparalleled restraint in expressing opinion regarding that country. This was attributed to the feeling in Pakistan that the policy of Afghanistan did not represent the true feelings of the Afghan people who, on the whole, remained friendly in spite of the constant hostile propaganda of their government. Pakistan's good sense has been rewarded by the betterment of official relations between the two countries.

The problem of national antipathy has only one facet. It arises in relations with India. Actually the people of Pakistan are willing to come to an honourable settlement with their neighbour in spite of the history of the last century, but they feel that their desire is not fully reciprocated. It would, therefore, be wrong to say that national antipathy towards India does not exist, but it can be easily removed if India adopts a conciliatory policy. The people of Pakistan feel that they have done everything in their power to create better feelings between themselves and India. Actually, even the most objective observers would say that this is a greater problem with India than with Pakistan. The Hindus and the Sikhs in India have shown such strong anti-Muslim bias that Pakistan would have to be populated with angels not to be affected by the Indian feeling. This is an unhealthy aspect of life in the Indo-Pakistan sub-continent and has dangerous potentialities. One can only hope that these difficulties will be removed and such relations as should subsist between neighbours will ultimately come to be established. At present, however, it seems that this will be impossible without the good offices of the United Nations. If those powers which fashion the policy of the United Nations do not realize the results of the growing antipathy between India and Pakistan, it may ultimately lead to disastrous consequences. It is obvious that the evil consequences of such a catastrophe cannot be localized in the Indo-Pakistan sub-continent. Even if they could, it should be remembered that a considerable part of humanity resides in this area. International opinion, therefore, must take an active interest in this situation.

Because of her geographical and strategic position and the potential dangers to which she is exposed, Pakistan naturally desires strong world affiliations. She has no aggressive designs against any country. All that she asks for is peace to build up her industrial and economic resources and to raise the standard of living of her people. Pakistan cannot make a contribution to the welfare of the world without peace. Nor can she achieve prosperity and 'good life' for her people unless the world is able to curb and suppress aggression. It is obvious, therefore, that it is the innermost desire of the people of Pakistan to see a tranquil, stable and united world.

It is not only in the realm of politics that a united world can bring happiness to younger and weaker nations; there are many avenues of constructive effort where world co-operation can bring about more enlightenment, better health and greater happiness to humanity. Pakistan is not only willing but anxious that this co-operation should become a living reality; in every sphere of human activity it is anxious to co-operate with the nations of the world, because in the welfare of the world lies her own future. This defines the attitude of the people of Pakistan towards the world community. Even dwellers in distant hamlets, whose knowledge is extremely limited, are desirous of peace and constructive effort; the objectives of the United Nations, therefore, command their sympathy. Only when they think that an unjust decision has been made or a just grievance has failed to find redress on account of powerful influences at work, do the Pakistanis feel disappointed. This disappointment also is a measure of their desire to see a world community united in constructive effort for eradicating injustice and devoting itself to the welfare of humanity.

Appendix

THE PRESENT STATE OF SCIENTIFIC RESEARCH ON THE QUESTIONS RAISED ABOVE

SOCIOLOGICAL studies have not made rapid strides in Pakistan. During the last few years it was with difficulty that Pakistan put her educational machinery into gear again. Even before the Partition international and sociological studies had not advanced greatly in the sub-continent of Indo-Pakistan. These subjects are taught up to the post-graduate level, but the amount of research has not been impressive. The Government of Pakistan, however, has published various reports which give figures of economic and sociological importance and the Publications Department of the Government has brought out some brochures, books and pamphlets. These are mostly of a factual nature and do not deal with all the subjects treated in this treatise. The following books contain useful information :

1. *Imperial Gazetteer of India* (for the areas now constituting Pakistan).
2. *The First Year* ⎫
3. *The Second Year* ⎪
4. *The Third Year* ⎬ Published by Pakistan Publications,
5. *The Fourth Year* ⎪ Karachi.
6. *The Fifth Year* ⎪
7. *The Sixth Year* ⎭
8. *Introducing Pakistan,* Pakistan Institute of International Affairs.
9. *An Introduction to Pakistan,* Maneck B. Pithawalla.
10. *Muslim League Yesterday and Today,* A. B. Rajput. Publishers, Muhammad Ashraf, Lahore.
11. *Whither Pakistan ?* Z. A. Suleri. Eastern Publishers, London, S.W.1.
12. *The Cultural Heritage of Pakistan,* S. M. Ikram and Percival Spear. Oxford University Press, London.

13. *Pakistan and the Middle East,* M. Ahmad, Kitabi Markaz, Karachi.

14. *Pakistan Hamara,* Fazl Ahmad Siddiqi.

15. *Muhajrin ka Masala,* Agha Mohammad Ashraf. Pakistan Publications, Karachi.

16. *The Development of Indo-Muslim Culture,* I. H. Qureshi. Muhammad Ashraf, Lahore.

17. *The Development of Islamic Polity,* I. H. Qureshi, Muhammad Ashraf, Lahore.

18. *Constituent Assembly Debates,* especially the debate on the Objectives Resolution.

19. *Pakistan Horizon* ⎫
20. *Muashiyat* ⎪
21. *Pakistan Quarterly* ⎬ Journals.
22. *Al-Bashir* ⎪
23. *Pakistan Review* ⎭

24. *Crescent and Green, a miscellany of writings on Pakistan.* Cassell & Co., London, 1955.

25. *Pakistan,* 1953–54 ⎫
26. *Pakistan,* 1954–55 ⎬ Pakistan Publications, Karachi.
27. *Pakistan,* 1955–56 ⎭

Select Bibliography

The Imperial Gazetteer of India, 2nd Ed. Vols. 1–4. Oxford, 1909.

Indian and Pakistan Yearbooks, 1948, 1949, 1950. *Times of India.*

Pakistan Yearbook, 1949, Kitabistan, Karachi, 1949.

Cambridge History of India, Vols. III, IV, and VI.

AHMAD, JAMIL-UD-DIN: *Speeches and Writings of Mr. Jinnah.* Lahore, Muhd. Ashraf, 1925. 2 Vols.

ALBIRUNI, A. H.: *Makers of Pakistan and Modern Muslim India*, Lahore, Muhd. Ashraf, 1950.

AKHTAR, S. M.: *Economics of Pakistan.* Lahore Publishers Ltd. 1951.

BOLITHO, HECTOR: *Jinnah.* John Murray, London.

BROWN, W. N.: *India, Pakistan and Ceylon.* Cornell University Press. 1951.

COUPLAND, R.: *The Indian Problem*, Oxford. 1942.

DAVIS, KINGSLEY: *The Population of India and Pakistan.* Princeton University Press. 1951.

GODFREY, WALTER: *Pakistan.* London, His Majesty's Stationery Office. 1951. Overseas Economic Surveys.

LIAQUAT ALI KHAN: *Pakistan, The Heart of Asia.* Cambridge, Harvard University Press. 1950.

RAVOOF, A. A.: *Meet Mr. Jinnah.* Lahore, Muhd. Ashraf. 1947.

SAIYID, M. H.: *Mohammad Ali Jinnah.* Lahore, Muhd. Ashraf. 1942.

SPEAR, PERCIVAL: *India, Pakistan and the West.* London, Oxford University Press. 1952.

STEPHENS, IAN : *The Horned Moon.* London, Chatto & Windus. 1953.

SYMONDS, RICHARD: *The Making of Pakistan.* London, Faber and Faber. 1949.

TUKER, SIR FRANCIS: *While Memory Serves.* London, Cassell and Co. 1950.

WHEELER, R. E. M.: *Five Thousand Years of Pakistan.* London, Royal India and Pakistan Society. 1950.

STATISTICS AND OTHER DOCUMENTS

Government of India Act, 1935, *as Adopted by the Pakistan (Provisional Constitution) Order, and Amended up to January* 1952. Government of Pakistan, Karachi. 1952.

Statistical Digest of Pakistan. Issued by the Department of Commercial Intelligence and Statistics, Government of Pakistan.

Statistical Bulletin. Published by Government of Pakistan.

The Constitution of the Islamic Republic of Pakistan. Government of Pakistan, Karachi. 1956.

Census Reports of Pakistan. Government of Pakistan, Karachi.

Index

Abbasids, 7
Abdur Rahim Khan Khanan, 7
Accession to Federation, 39
Administrative organization, 37, *et seq.*
Adult education, 32, *also see* Education.
Adult franchise, 40, 42
Afghan, 3, 9
Afghanistan, 65, 72
Agent to Governor General, 39
Agrarian administration, 36
Agrarian reform, 53, 59
Agriculture, 3, 20, 47, 48, 50, 51
Agriculturists, 4
Ajanta, 10
Akbar, 7, 8
Alberuni, 7
Ambassadors, 38
America, 56
Americans, 72
Amir Khusraw, *see* Khusraw.
Arabia, 15
Arabic, 1, 2, 8, 9, 11, 12, 25, 27
Arabs, 6, 7, 9, 24, 47, 64
Architecture, 10, 14
Art, 10, 16
Artisans, 4, *also see* Craftsmen.
Aryan, 1, 24, 61, 62
Australia, 5

Bahawalpur, 38, 39, 53
Baluch, 2, 4
Baluchi, 1
Baluchistan, 1, 38, 39, 56, 64
Barmecides, 7
Basket-ball, 34
Belgium, 56
Bengal, 3, 8, 52, 53, 56, *also see* East Bengal, East Pakistan, Eastern Pakistan.
Bengali, 1, 2, 3, 8, 38
Bhakti Marga, 62
Bhakti movement, 7
Birth and rebirth, doctrine of, 61, 62, 63
Bombay, 49, 50
Brahma, 63
Brahminism, 61, 62, 63, *also see* Hinduism.
Brahmins, 63, 64, 65
Britain, 53, *also see* British.

British, 2, 3, 4, 10, 20, 25, 26, 30, 36, 37, 38, 39, 46, 48, 49, 57
British Parliament, 38
Brohi, 1
Buddha, 63
Buddhism, 24, 63, *also see* Buddhists.
Buddhists, 64, 65, 67, *also see* Buddhism.
Bureaucracy, 8, 35, 36, *also see* Public Servants.
Burma, 72

Cabinet, 38, 39, 40, 41, 42, *also see* Ministers.
Calcutta, 39, 49, 50
Caste, 19, 44, 62, 63, 66
Catholics, 64, 68
Cement, 55
Central government, 69
Certiorari, 42
Ceylon, 72
Chaghtai, 16
Chaupals, 20
Chief Minister, 39, 42
China, 47
Chitral, 38
Chittagong, 39, 55
Christ, 65
Christian, 18, 21, 64, 66, 67, 69
Christianity, 10
Christian missionaries, 21
Christian women, 21, *also see* Women.
Chromite, 56
Clubs, 20
Coal, 56
College, 25, 28, 31
Colour consciousness, 6, 62
Commerce, 57, *also see* Trade
Commonwealth, 43, 44
Communists, 58, 59
Constituent assembly, 38, 39, *also see* First Constituent Assembly, Second Constituent Assembly.
Constitution, 38, 40, 41, 42, 43
Conversion, 6, 10, 64, 65
Co-operative cultivation, 53
Cornwallis, 52
Cottage industries, 52, *also see* Crafts, Handicrafts and Craftsmen.
Cotton mills, 49, 50, 53

79

Crafts, 20, *also see* Handicrafts, Cottage Industries and Craftsmen.
Craftsmen, 4, 16, 17, 18, 57, 58
Cricket, 34
Culture, Chapter I, 5, 6, 7, 9, 10, 11, 12, 13, 22, 24, 26, 71, *also see* Indo-Muslim culture and Muslim civilization.

Dacca, 24, 48, 49
Dargai, 56
Delhi sultanate, 8
Devanagri, 11
Dir, 38
Distribution of income, 57
Dominions, 38
Dravidian, 1, 6

East Bengal, 1, 38, 39, 40, 50, *also see* Bengal and Eastern Pakistan.
East Pakistan, Eastern Pakistan, 1, 2, 30, 41, 42, 45, 48, 51, 59, 64, 65, 66, 71
Education, 3, 4, 8, 12, 13, 20, 21, 22, Chapter III, 24–34, 49
Egypt, 47
Election commission, 42
English, 2
Ethical principles, 16
Ethnical groups, 5
Europe, 47
European, 6, 72
European music, 10

Factories, 48, *also see* Industrial Development.
Family, Chapter II, 17, 18
Federal capital, 1, 38, 41, *also see* Karachi.
Federal jurisdiction, 42
Federal Parliament, 2, 41, *also see* Parliament, National Assembly.
Federation, 38, 39, 45
Fertilizers, 5
Feudalism, 35
Film industry, 33
First Constituent Assembly, 40, 45
First Five Year Plan, 59
Firuz Shah, 7
Floud commission, 53
Food, 58
Football, 34
Foreign capital, 55, 57
Foreigners, 71
Franchise, *see* Adult Franchise.
Free enterprise, 54, 58

Fundamental education, 32
Fundamental rights, 42

Games, 34, *also see* Sport.
Gaur, 24
Ghazal, 10
Ghaznawids, 24, 60, 61
Ghulam Muhammad, 45
Gñana Marga, 62
Goa, 64
Government of India Act, 1919...37
Government of India Act, 1935...37, 38
Governor, 31, 39, 41
Governor General, 38, 40, 45
Great Britain, 38
Greeks, 7
Guilds, 58
Gypsum, 56

Habeas corpus, 42
Handicrafts, 48, 49, *also see* Crafts and Craftsmen.
Harappa, 24, 35, 61
Hari Haqdar, 58
Hebrew prophets, 65
High Courts, 42
Hinayana, 63
Hindi, 7, 8
Hindi poetry, 7
Hindu culture, 7, *also see* Culture.
Hinduism, 5, 7, 8, 9, 10, 12, 17, 64, *also see* Brahminism.
Hindu music, 9
Hindus, 4, 6, 7, 8, 9, 10, 13, 18, 19, 21, 30, 44, 46, 57, 62, 63, 64, 65, 66, 70, 73
Hindu scriptures, 8
Hindu women, 19, 21, 22, *also see* Women.
Hindwi, 8
Hockey, 34
Home, 20
Hyderabad, 54

Impeachment, 41
Independence Act, 1947...38
India, 6, 7, 9, 11, 12, 13, 33, 35, 38, 39, 46, 47, 48, 49, 50, 69, 72, 73, *also see* Indo-Pakistan sub-continent.
Indian Islam, 5, 6, 8, 10, 11, 14, 15, 16, 18, 24, *also see below.*
Indian Muslims, 9, 11, 12, 13, 72
Indian Ocean, 48
Individual, 16
Individual liberty, 71, *also see* Fundamental rights.

Indo-Aryans, 62
Indo-Muslim culture, 11, 12, *also see* Indian Islam.
Indo-Pakistan subcontinent, 4, 5, 24, 35, 36, 37, 47, 49, 73, *also see* India.
Indus, 5
Industrial development, 53, 54, 55, 56, *also see* Pakistan Industrial Development Corporation.
Industrial estates, 54, 55
Industrial Finance Corporation, 54
Industrialists, 66
Industrialization, 3
Industrial potential, 53
Industry, 4, 47, 48, 49, 70
Instrument of accession, 39, *also see* accession to Federation.
Iqbal, 16
Iran, 1
Iron, 56
Irrigation, 51, 52, 53
Islam, 4, 5, 6, 7, 8, 9, 11, 14, 18, 24, 39, 43, 64, 65, 66, 67, 68, *also see* Indian-Islam.
Islamic culture, 14, *also see* Indo-Muslim civilization and Indo-Muslim culture.
Islamic provisions in constitution, 43
Islamic system of education, 24–26

Jagirdari, 52
Jainism, 63
Jews, 7, 67
Jihad Movement, 3
Jirgas, 38
Joint family, 19, 20
Judiciary, 42
Jurisprudence, 35
Jute mills, 49, 50, 55

Kabir, 7
Kalat, 38
Karachi, 32, 38, 41, 54, 64, *also see* Federal capital.
Karma Marga, 62
Karnaphuli, 56
Karta, 19
Kashmir, 48, 70, 72
Khadijah, 16
Khairpur, 38, 39
Khulna, 56
Khusraw, 7
Kitab-ul-Hind, 7
Kshatriyas, 63

Labour unions, 59
Labour unrest, 59
Lahore, 3, 24, 25, 65

Landlords, 37, 44, 51, 52, 53, 58, 59
Languages, 1, 2, 13, 39, 71
Las Bela, 38
Leftist tendencies, 58
Legal system, 14
Legislatures, 37, 39, 41, *also see* Provincial legislature, Provincial Assembly, National Assembly, Parliament.
Liaquat Ali Khan, 67
Liberalism, 14
Linguistic groups, 1, 2, 4, 5
Literature, 16
Lower Sind Barrage, 53

Macaulay, 26
Mahavira, 63
Mahayana, 63, 65
Mahmud (of Ghaznih), 7
Makran, 38
Makrani, 1
Malakand, 56
Malik Muhammad Jaisi, 7
Mansura, 24
Maratha, 10
Mardan, 55
Matches, 55
Merchants, 66
Migration, 70
Minimum holding of agricultural land, 53
Ministers, 38, 41, 42, 67, *also see* Cabinet, Chief Minister, Prime Minister.
Minorities, 14, 43, 68
Mobile cinema vans, 34
Mobile schools, 32
Modernists, 40
Mohenjodaro, 24, 35, 61
Mosque, 67
Mughuls, 9, 10
Mughul Empire, 8, 10, 24
Muhammad, 15, 65
Muhammad bin Bakhtyar Khalji, 65
Muhammad bin Qasim, 7
Multan, 24, 65
Muslim architecture, 9
Muslim civilization, 6
Muslim countries, 72
Muslim cuisine, 9
Muslim League Party, 40
Muslim music, 9
Muslim peoples, 5
Muslims, 3, 4, 5, 6, 7, 8, 9, 10, 12, 13, 21, 25, 30, 35, 66, 67
Muslim women, 21, *also see* Women.
Mymensingh, 3

National Assembly, 41, 42, *also see* Parliament.

Nationalism, 4, 5, 13
Nationalization of industry, 58
National unity, 71
Natural gas, 56
Naushehra, 56
Negro, 6
New Zealand, 56
Nirvana, 63
Non-Muslims, 43, 45, *also see* Christians, Hindus, Jews, Scheduled castes, Zoroastrians, etc.
North-west Frontier, 2, 52, 53, 56, 71
North-west Frontier Province, 31, 38, 51

Olympic Association, 34
Outcastes, 63

Painters, 16
Pakistan Industrial Development Corporation, 54
Panjab, *see* Punjab.
Panjabi, 1, 2, 3
Paper mill, 55
Pardah, 22, *see also* Veil.
Parliament, 38, 42, *also see* National Assembly.
Pathan, 1, 2, 3
Path of action, 62
Path of devotion, 62
Path of knowledge, 62
Peasant organizations, 58
Peasant proprietors, 37, 51, 53
Peasants, 17, 18, 44, 51, 58, 59, 66
Permanent settlement, 52, 53
Persian, 1, 2, 7, 8, 9, 12, 25, 27
Personnel of services, 37, 58
Petroleum, 56
Phallic worship, 63
Physical education, 34
Planning of industries, 58
Poets, 16
Political awakening, 32, 33, *also see* below.
Political consciousness, 46
Political maturity, 46
Political organization, 32, 33
Politics, 46
Polity, 46
Polo, 34
Polyandry, 18
Polygamy, 18
Prakrit, 8, 9, 11
President, 41, 42, 43
Press, 34
Priesthood, 14
Priests, 15

Prime Minister, 42
Princely States, 38, 39, 40
Princes, 39, *also see below.*
Protestants, 64
Provinces, 40, 41
Provincial Assemblies, 41, 42
Provincial autonomy, 38
Provincial government, 41
Provincial jurisdiction, 42, 43
Provincial legislature, 40, 41
Public servants, 4, 36
Public Services Commission, 42
Pubs, 20
Pukhtu, 1
Pukhtun, 1
Punjab, 1, 24, 38, 48, 51, 52, 56, 61, 65
Pushtu, 1

Qaid-i-Azam, 67
Qawwali, 1
Queen, 38, 43
Quo warranto, 42
Qur'an, 24, 65

Racial feeling, 6
Racial types, 1
Radio, 33
Railways, 5, 48, 57
Rajput, 10, 35
Rasul, 56
Raw materials, 53, 54
Refugees, 4, 23, 46, 69
Regional patriotism, 71
Religion, 20, 26, *see also* Islam, Buddhism, Christianity, Hinduism.
Religious education, 28
Republic, 43
Restaurants, 20
Revivalism, 10, 11, 12, 13
Roman, 36

Saiyid Ahmad Shahid, 3
Saljuqs, 65
Sanskrit, 7, 9, 11, 27
Scheduled castes, 66, 67
Scholars, 16
Schools, 20, 25, 27, 31
Science, 28
Scientists, 16
Script, 11
Second Constituent Assembly, 40
Secretariat, 40
Sehwan, 24
Self immolation, 63
Shaivite worship, 61
Shiva, 61, 63

Shoe industry, 55
Sialkot, 56
Sikandar Lodi, 7, 8
Sikhs, 10, 73
Sind, 1, 7, 24, 38, 51, 52, 64, 65
Sindhi, 1, 2, 4
Smaller industries, 56
Social justice, 14, 45, 58
Social system, 12
Soldiers, 2, 3, 4
Speaker, 42
Sport, 34
Standard of living, 57, 58
Strawboard, 56
Students, 25, 29, 30, 32, 59
Subinfeudation, 59
Sudras, 63
Sugar, 55
Sultanate of Delhi, 65
Surgical instruments, 56
Swat, 38
Switzerland, 56
Sylhet, 56

Takshashila, 24
Tantrism, 63, 64
Taxila, 24, 35
Teachers, 4, 24, 28, 29, 30, 31, 32
Technical education, 28, 31
Tenancy Laws, 53
Tenants, 52
Tennis, 34
Textiles, 55
Thal Project, 53
Thatta, 24
Theocracy, 14, 15, 46
Theology, 25, 28
Tobacco, 56
Tolerance, 10, 14, 15, 45
Totalitarian tendencies, 70
Towns, 35
Trade, 39, 47, *also see* Commerce.
Trade unions, 59
Traditionalists, 40

Tribal areas, 39, 40, 41
Tribal territories, 38
Tribes, 20, 31, 71
Turkish, 8, 9
Turks, 3, 7, 9, 65

Unemployment, 53
U.N.E.S.C.O., 32
United Front, 40
United Kingdom, 38, 43
United Nations, 33, 44, 73, 74
Universities, 26, 27, 28, 29, 31
Untouchability, 10
Urdu, 1, 2
Vaishyas, 63
Vama-margi, 63
Varna, 62, *also see* Caste.
Vedas, 20, 61
Veil, 21, 22, *also see* Pardah.
Village, 35, 47
Village, A.I.D. Programme, 32
Vishnu, 63
Vocational training, 3, 31, *also see* Technical education.
Volley ball, 34

Warsak, 56
Western Asia, 48
Westernization, 13
West Pakistan, Western Pakistan, 1, 2, 5, 30, 40, 41, 42, 45, 49, 50, 51, 56, 59
Women, 19, 21
Woollen mills, 56
Workers, 32, 44, 58, 59, 66
Workers' right of organization, 58
Workers' rights, 58
Wrestling, 34
Writers, 16

Zoroaster, Zoroastrians, 64, 66

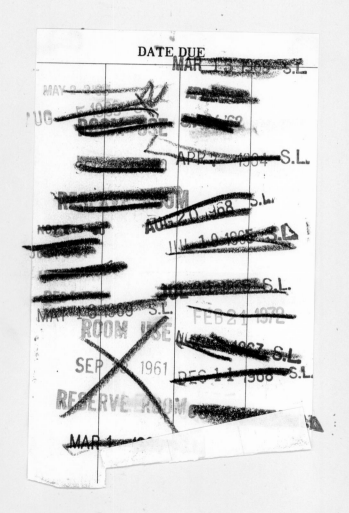

DATE DUE